MS-Works

Made Simple

Made Simple *Computer Books*

- easy to follow
- jargon free
- practical
- task based
- easy steps

All you want are the **basics**. You don't want to be bothered with all the advanced stuff, or be engulfed in technical mumbo jumbo. You have neither the time nor the interest in knowing about every feature, function or command and you don't want to wade through big computer books on the subject or stumble through the maze of information in the manuals.

The **MADE SIMPLE** series is **for you!**

You want to **learn quickly what's essential** and **how** to do things with a particular piece of software. You are:

- **a Secretary** or temp who wants to **get the job done**, **quickly** and **efficiently**

- **a Manager**, without the time to learn all about the software but who wants to **produce letters, memos, reports** or **spreadsheets**

- someone **working from home**, who needs a **self-teaching** approach, that gives **results fast**, with the least confusion.

By a combination of **tutorial approach**, with **tasks to do**, and **easy steps**, the **MADE SIMPLE** series of Computer Books stands above all others.

See the complete series at your **local bookshop now**, or in case of difficulty, contact:

Reed Book Services Ltd., Orders Dept, PO Box 5, Rushden, Northants, NN10 9YX. Tel 0933 58521. Fax 0933 50284. Credit card sales 0933 410511.

Series titles:

AmiPro	Moira Stephen	0 7506 2067 6
Excel	Stephen Morris	0 7506 2070 6
Lotus 1-2-3	Ian Robertson	0 7506 2066 8
MS-DOS	Ian Sinclair	0 7506 2069 2
MS-Works	P. K. McBride	0 7506 2065 X
Windows	P. K. McBride	0 7506 2072 2
Word	Keith Brindley	0 7506 2071 4
WordPerfect	Stephen Copestake	0 7506 2068 4

MS-Works
Made Simple

P.K.McBride

MADE SIMPLE
BOOKS

Made Simple
An imprint of Butterworth-Heinemann Ltd
Linacre House, Jordan Hill, Oxford OX2 8DP

ℛ   A member of the Reed Elsevier plc group

OXFORD   LONDON   BOSTON
MUNICH   NEW DELHI   SINGAPORE   SYDNEY
TOKYO   TORONTO   WELLINGTON

First published 1994
Reprinted 1995 (twice)

ISBN 0 7506 2065 X

🍄 Typeset by P.K.McBride, Southampton
Archtype, Bash Casual, Cotswold and Gravity fonts from Advanced Graphics Ltd
Icons designed by Sarah Ward © 1994
Printed and bound in Great Britain
by Scotprint, Musselburgh, Scotland

Contents

Preface

The computer is about as simple as a spacecraft, and who ever let an untrained spaceman loose? You pick up a manual that weighs more than your birth-weight, open it and find that its written in computerspeak. You see messages on the screen that look like code and the thing even makes noises. No wonder that you feel it's your lucky day if everything goes right. What do you do if everything goes wrong? Give up.

Training helps. Being able to type helps. Experience helps. This book helps, by providing training and assisting with experience. It can't help you if you always manage to hit the wrong keys, but it can tell you which are the right ones and what to do when you hit the wrong ones. After some time, even the dreaded manual will start to make sense, just because you know what the writers are wittering on about.

Computing is not black magic. You don't need luck or charms, just a bit of understanding. The problem is that the programs that are used nowadays look simple but aren't. Most of them are crammed with features you don't need – but how do you know what you don't need? This book shows you what is essential and guides you through it. You will know how to make an action work and why. The less essential bits can wait – and once you start to use a program with confidence you can tackle these bits for yourself.

The writers of this series have all been through it. We know your time is valuable, and you don't want to waste it. You don't buy books on computer subjects to read jokes or be told that you are a dummy. You want to find what you need and be shown how to achieve it. Here, at last, you can.

1 Starting work

Great works ...

Word Processor

Use this to write your letters, reports, newsletters and novels. The range of facilities on offer almost makes this a desktop publishing package. There are a wide range of typefaces, font styles and sizes, to be used for headings and for emphasis; headers, footers and page numbers can be added; text can be laid out in columns; and graphics, charts and tables can be placed in the text.

Spreadsheet

Use this to manage your cheque book, payroll, cash flow and all other aspects of your accounts – or anything else that involves numbers and calculations. With its DTP facilities, you can also use this for invoices and estimates. It doesn't have the 3-D features that are present in the latest full-cost packages, but it should be capable of handling all the number-crunching requirements of a small business or home user.

Database

Use this to manage your stock, organize your address book or any other sets of data. If any calculations are needed, this will produce a range of summary values, and data can be easily transferred between here and the spreadsheet.

Communications

With this, you can send and receive documents of all types over the phone lines (as long as you own a modem).

... and lesser works

- ❑ These can only be used from within one of the major tools.

ClipArt manages a gallery of graphics that can be placed in documents. Some pictures are supplied with Works, and you can add your own graphics or bought-in Clip Art to the gallery.

Draw is a graphics program, with a similar set of tools to those in the Windows Paintbrush, though Draw works in a rather different way.

Take note

In Works, a Tool means one of the major or minor programs listed here; a Document means any text or data file created by one of the Tools.

Integration

Graph lets you produce pie charts, line, bar and other more exotic graphs, from sets of figures in a spreadsheet or database.

Note-It lets you add comments to any text document. These are tucked out of the way and only shown when the reader clicks on a Note-it symbol.

Word-Art lets you create special text effects, such as slanting or curved text, perhaps with shadows or other trimmings, for labels and headings.

Works is an integrated suite, developed for the SoHo market. Let's try that again in English... Works is a set of programs, designed for the Small Office/Home Office users. The integration works at three levels.

● All use the same common set of core commands, so that when you have mastered one program, you are half way to mastery of the next.

● Any number of documents, from the same or different tools, can be in use at the same, so that you can flick quickly from one job to another.

● Data can be transferred freely between them, so that charts created from a spreadsheet can be copied into a report; lists of names and addresses, organised in the database can be merged with a standard letter to produce a customised mailing; word-processed memos can be taken into communications and zipped off down the phone line.

Tip

Get to grips with the Word Processor first, then move on to the Spreadsheet, before you try the Database — it is the trickiest of these three.

Starting work

When you first come into Works, and whenever you set out to create a new document, you will meet the **Startup** dialog box. What better place to start our trip around the Works.

As it says on the box, this is where you create a **New** or open on of your **Recent Documents**, but you can also switch from here to:

- **Open an Existing Document.** This takes you to a dialog box in which you can browse through your directories to select an older file. The recently used ones will also be there, but can be opened more quickly from the list in the Startup dialog box.

- **Use a Template.** Templates are ready-formatted blank documents into which you can write your own data. They cover a good range of common tasks such as invoices, inventories, resumes and budgetting. Spreadsheet templates have all the necessary formulae built into them; all have text styles, colours and layouts ready set. They are well designed and easy to use. If you really want things *made simple* for you, use templates. (See page 12.)

- **Use a Works Wizard.** Here's something else not to be missed by *made simple* enthusiasts. Wizards create documents, covering a wider range of tasks than those of the templates. All you have to do is make a few choices about layout, styles and decorations on the documents. (See page 14.)

- **Instructions.** This simply displays brief notes about the Startup options.

Basic steps

- ❑ To create a New document:

1 Click on the icon for the type of document that you want to create.

2 Click **OK** to confirm.

- ❑ To open a Recent Document:

1 Click on its name in the **Recent** list - if it is there.

2 Click **OK** to confirm.

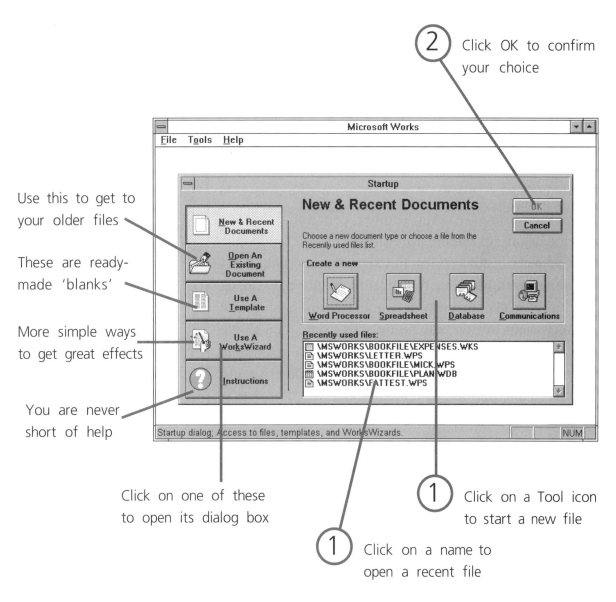

② Click OK to confirm your choice

Use this to get to your older files

These are ready-made 'blanks'

More simple ways to get great effects

You are never short of help

Click on one of these to open its dialog box

① Click on a Tool icon to start a new file

① Click on a name to open a recent file

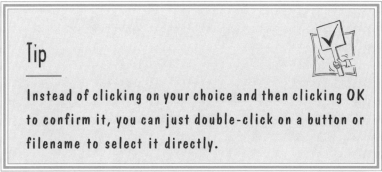

Tip

Instead of clicking on your choice and then clicking OK to confirm it, you can just double-click on a button or filename to select it directly.

5

The desktop

Think of the Works screen as your desktop.

The main area – the **Workspace** – is where you lay out your documents. Each of these is in its own window, which can be minimised out of the way, or tucked beneath or to the side of the one you are currently working on.

Above the workspace is the **Toolbar**, containing buttons which can call up the most frequently used commands. Most aspects of font styles and settings, and alignment can be set from here. If a button is highlighted, it means that its setting is currently active. In the screenshot, the Left alignment button is the only active one. As a single click on one of these will replace two or three selections through menus, they are well worth using. You can add buttons to the Toolbar, or remove those you do not use. (See *Customising the Toolbar*, page 10.)

At the top of the screen is the **Menu Bar**, and the menus that can be pulled down from here, carry the full range of commands. The contents of the menu bar vary slightly from one tool to another. (See *The menu system*, page 8.)

At the bottom of the screen is the **Status Bar**. When you are selecting from menus or the toolbar buttons, this carries brief reminders of the purpose of the commands.

Tip

Hold the pointer for a moment over the toolbar icons, and a *Tool Tip* will appear to tell you what the icon does.

Toolbar

Font name and size

Tool Tip

Menu Bar

Highlighted means active

Workspace

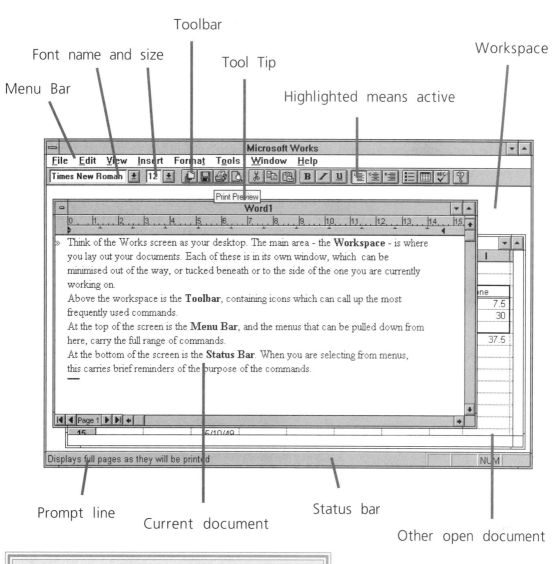

Prompt line

Current document

Status bar

Other open document

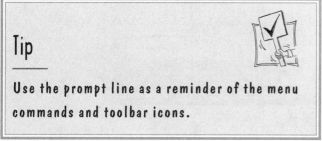

Tip

Use the prompt line as a reminder of the menu commands and toolbar icons.

The menu system

All of Works' facilities can be accessed through the menu system. The commands are grouped under more-or-less appropriate headings. The fit isn't quite perfect because not every command falls into a neat category. But finding a command is rarely a problem.

If you see a **tick** to the left of a menu option, it means that this is a toggle (on/off) switch, and that it is currently turned on.

If you see an ellipsis (...) after a menu option, selecting this will open a dialog box in which you will give further information or make detailed selections.

❑ **To select a command:**

1 Point to a heading in the Menu bar and its menu will drop down.

2 If you do not see what you want, move the pointer along, opening other menus.

3 When you find the comand you want, click to select it.

❑ **To abandon selection:**

4 Click anywhere else on screen to close the menu.

① Click on a heading to open its menu

③ Click on the option

Toggle switch - this one is on

This calls up a dialog box

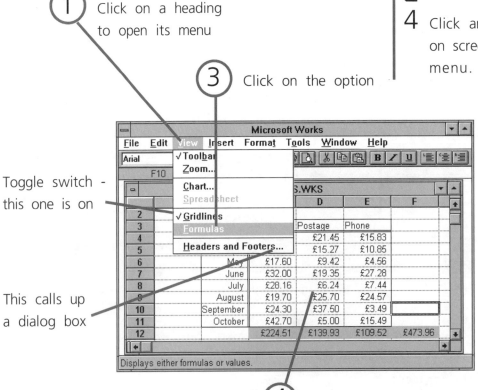

④ Click off the menu to abandon

Basic steps

Selecting with keys

☐ **To select a command:**

1 Press **[Alt]**. This tells the system to expect a key selection.

2 Press the underlined letter of the header to open the menu.

3 Press the underlined letter of the menu option.

☐ **To abandon selection:**

4 Press **[Esc]**.

When you are typing in data, it is sometimes simpler to make your menu selections with the keys, rather than with the mouse. Some of the more commonly used commands have **[Ctrl]** key combination shortcuts, but all can be accessed via the **[Alt]** key.

The quickest method is to use the key letter of the menu choices, but if you want to browse, or use the **[Left]** and **[Right]** arrow keys to move along the menu bar and the **[Up]** and **[Down]** arrows to move the highlight to the option you want. Pressing **[Enter]** selects the highlighted option.

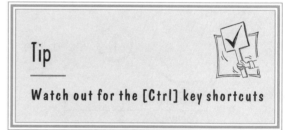

Tip
_____

Watch out for the [Ctrl] key shortcuts

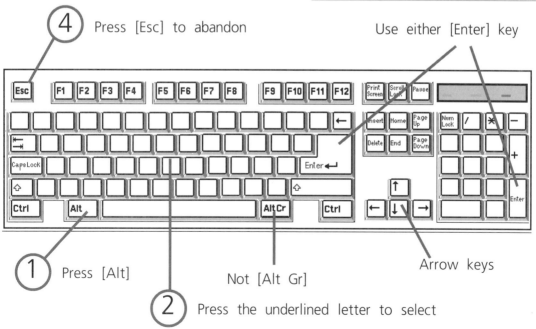

④ Press [Esc] to abandon

Use either [Enter] key

① Press [Alt]

Not [Alt Gr]

Arrow keys

② Press the underlined letter to select

Customising the toolbar

Any time that you are working on a document, you can change the contents of the toolbar, adding or removing buttons. The changes that you make will be there whenever you use the same tool. So, if you add a Tab control button while working on a word processor document, it will be there for all word processor documents in future, though not for other Tools.

The **Customize Toolbar** dialog box also carries an option to **Remove Font Name and Point Size**. If you are not making regular use of these, clearing them away will leave more space for extra buttons.

❑ **To add a button:**

1 Open the **Tools** menu and select **Customize Toolbar...**

2 At the dialog box, select the **Category** (the menu heading).

3 Select the desired button and drag it onto the toolbar.

4 Release it wherever you want it to fit. The others will shuffle up to make room.

5 Click **OK** to confirm.

❑ **To remove a button:**

1 Open the **Customize Toolbar** dialog box.

2 Select the unwanted button and drag it back into the box.

3 Click **OK** to confirm.

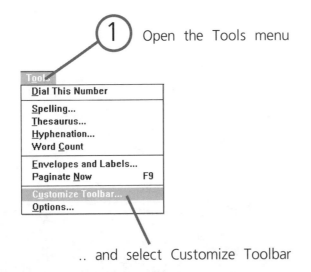

Open the Tools menu

.. and select Customize Toolbar

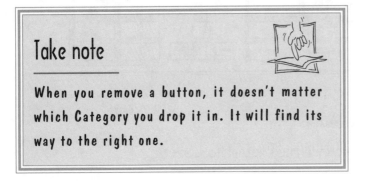

Take note

When you remove a button, it doesn't matter which Category you drop it in. It will find its way to the right one.

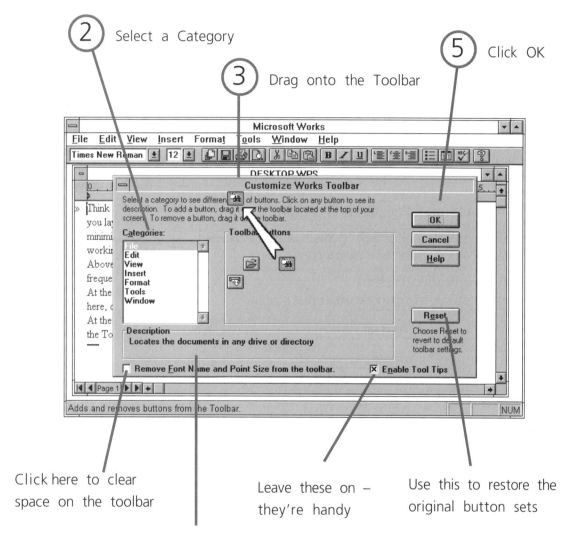

② Select a Category

③ Drag onto the Toolbar

⑤ Click OK

Click here to clear space on the toolbar

Leave these on – they're handy

Use this to restore the original button sets

This tells you what the button does

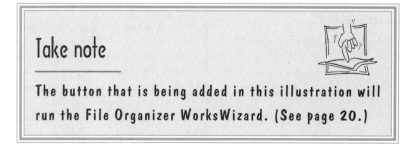

Take note

The button that is being added in this illustration will run the File Organizer WorksWizard. (See page 20.)

Using templates

Check the Templates befor you start on a new spreadsheet, database or word processor document. There may be one there that will do the job. Even if the template is not exactly what you need, it may be quicker to adapt one of these, than to create a new document from scratch.

There are over 30 templates, arranged into three main groups, subdivided into categories:

Business
- Billing – invoices and accounts
- Planning – budgets and cash flow
- Documents – fax cover and newletter
- Expenses – purchase order
- Inventory – stock list and vendors database
- Management – customer, employee and contacts lists, and time sheet
- Sales – estimates, orders and price list.

Personal
- Addresses – personal and club membership
- Documents – resume
- Household Management – book, CD, video and recipe collections
- Personal Finance – loan analysis, credit card database and financial statement

Education
- Classroom Management – record keeping
- Productivity – grades and timetable
- Testing – essay and multiple choice questions

Basic steps

1 Select **Use a Template** from the Startup dialog box, or open the **File** menu and select **Templates**.

2 Select the **Group**, the **Category** and finally the **Template**.

3 Click **OK**.

4 When you have added your data, save it with a new name. (See *Saving files*, page 16.)

Take note

Templates always turn on the Cue Card help facility. See *Cue Cards*, page 28.

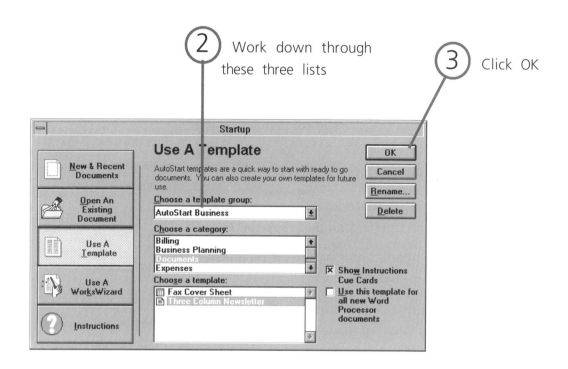

② Work down through these three lists

③ Click OK

Startup

Use A Template

AutoStart templates are a quick way to start with ready to go documents. You can also create your own templates for future use.

Choose a template group:

AutoStart Business ▼

Choose a category:

Billing
Business Planning
Documents
Expenses

Choose a template:

🖩 Fax Cover Sheet
📄 Three Column Newsletter

New & Recent Documents

Open An Existing Document

Use A Template

Use A WorksWizard

Instructions

OK
Cancel
Rename...
Delete

☒ Show Instructions Cue Cards

☐ Use this template for all new Word Processor documents

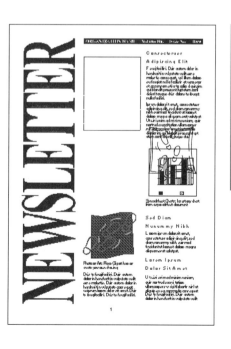

Most templates carry clear and copious instructions. Some, like the Newsletter shown here, have demostration text and graphics. The usefulness of the word processor templates lies in the fact that they have well-designed layouts and choice of fonts, styles and sizes; with the database templates you also have the data structure, and the spreadsheets have the calculations.

Using WorksWizards

WorksWizards are mini-programs that perform a variety of tasks. Most of them create databases of one sort or another. You finish up with a template, but you take an active part in the process of creation – choosing from a selection of styles, adding ClipArt, deciding which items to include in the database.

Three of the WorksWizards are different:

- Form Letter creates a standard letter for mail merging. We will return to this in Mail merge, page 133.

- Letterhead creates headed notepaper for business or home use. (See opposite.)

- File organizer is a utility for finding, renaming, copying and moving files. Most of these jobs can be done just as well with the Windows File Manager, but the find routines are excellent. (See pages 20.)

Basic steps

1 In the **Startup** dialog box, click on **Use WorksWizards...**

or

Open the **File** menu and select **WorksWizards...**

2 Click on the name in the **Choose** list.

3 Click **OK**.

4 Follow the prompts and make your selections as you work through the Wizard.

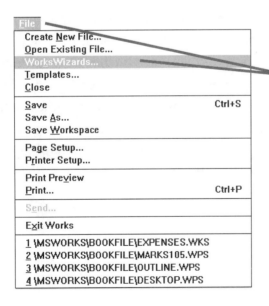

Select WorksWizards from the File menu

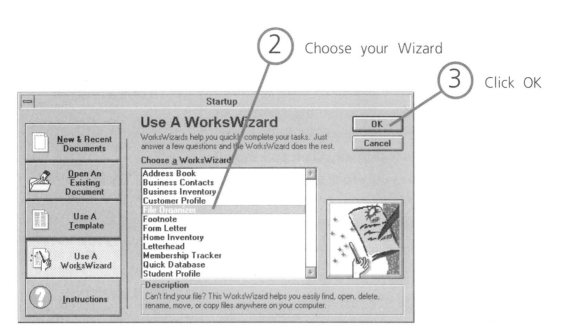

② Choose your Wizard

③ Click OK

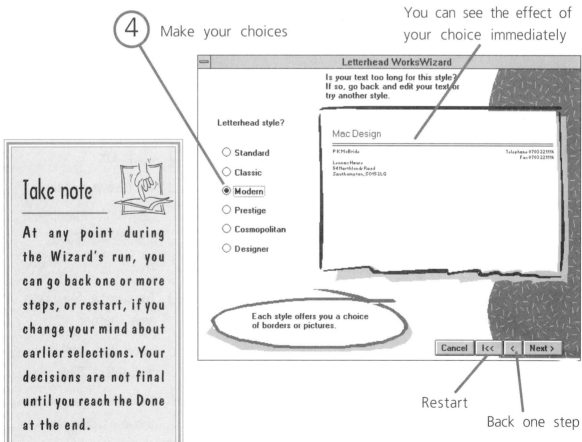

④ Make your choices

You can see the effect of your choice immediately

Restart

Back one step

Take note

At any point during the Wizard's run, you can go back one or more steps, or restart, if you change your mind about earlier selections. Your decisions are not final until you reach the Done at the end.

Saving files

While you are working on a document, its data is stored in the computer's memory. When you exit from Works, or switch of the machine, the memory is wiped. Sometimes, that can be a good thing. Do you really want to keep all those Thank You letters that you wrote after last Christmas? As long as you have sent printed copies off to your friends and relatives, you have no further use of them.

More often, perhaps, you will want to keep a copy of the document for reference, or to do some more work on in future. To do this, you must save it to disk.

The process is the same, whatever the type of document, and very simple. All you really have to do is decide on which disk and in which directory it will be stored, and what you will call it.

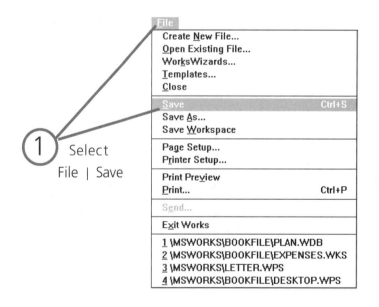

Select
File | Save

❏ **To save a new file:**

1 Open the **File** menu and select **Save**.

2 The first time you save a file, the **Save As** dialog box will appear to collect the details.

3 Select the **Drive** and the **Directory**.

4 Leave the **File Type** alone, unless you want to export the document for use with a different software package.

5 Type in a **File Name**.

6 Click **OK**.

❏ **To resave a file:**

1 Open the **File** menu and select **Save**.

2 That's it.

❏ **To save a file under a new name:**

1 Open the **File** menu and select **Save** As.

2 Fill in the details as above, typing in a new name.

Extensions

- The **Works** extensions:

wps Word Processor

wdb Database

wks Spreadsheet

wcm Communications

- Other extensions that you may meet:

wmf Windows MetaFile (for Clip Art)

bmp BitMap from Paintbrush or other art programs

txt Text file from Write, and other word processors

exe Executable programs. Never fiddle with these!

Take note

If you have edited a document and want to keep a copy of te original, as well as the new version, use **Save As** and give it a different name.

Filenames

There are two parts to every filename – the **name** itself and a three-letter **extension**. The name is given by you to a file when you save it.

There are a few limitations on filenames. They must not:

- be more than 8 characters long;
- contain spaces or punctuation;
- be the same as an existing file in the same directory (or the new will overwrite the old).

Most of all, the filename must *mean something to you*.

Don't bother about the extension. Leave it to Works to add a suitable one to identify the nature of the file.

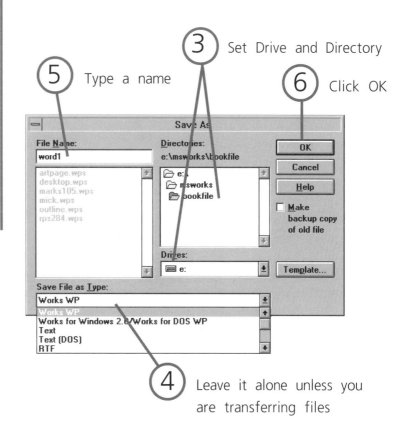

③ Set Drive and Directory

⑤ Type a name

⑥ Click OK

④ Leave it alone unless you are transferring files

Opening files

To get your documents back at the start of your next working session, you must open their files. Opening them is easy enough. The tricky part may well be *finding* them, especially as time goes by and your files start to run into their hundreds. However, Works goes a long way to make even this relatively painless.

Basic steps

1 Open the **File** menu and select **Open** or, click the Open button in the **Startup** dialog box.

2 Set the **Drive** and **Directory**, if necessary.

3 Pull down the **Type of files** list and select the type you want.

4 Scroll through the **Files** list and highlight the one you want.

5 Click **OK**.

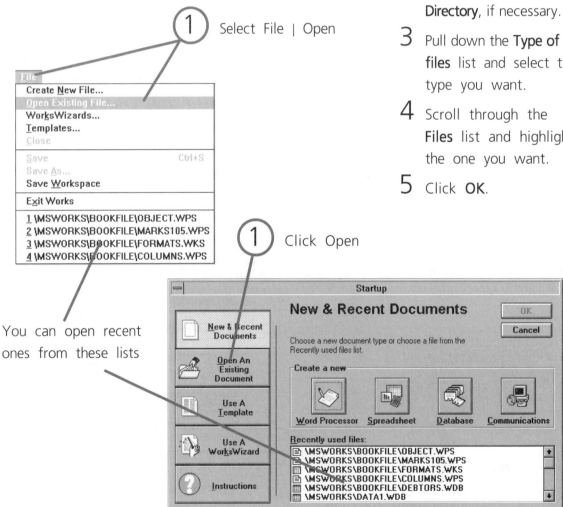

Select File | Open

Click Open

You can open recent ones from these lists

Transferring files?

❑ If you want to transfer the file to or from another machine, running different software, check the alternative file types. There is probably one there that will do the job.

Word processor documents can be saved and opened as plain Text or in Word, Wordperfect and other formats.

Spreadsheets can be saved or opened as Text or in Excel or Lotus 1-2-3 formats.

Databases can be saved or opened as Text, Comma Separated Text or in dBase formats.

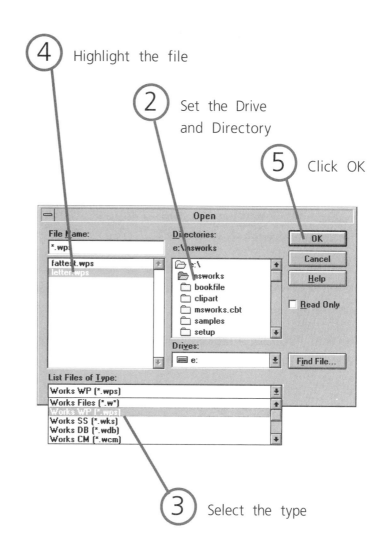

④ Highlight the file

② Set the Drive and Directory

⑤ Click OK

③ Select the type

Tip

If you cannot remember where you stored a file, click on the Find File button to open the File Organizer. (See next page.)

File organizer

Though this is a WorksWizard, it can also be added as a toolbar button, and accessed through the Find File button in the Open File dialog box. Its main value is that it can track down misplaced files, searching on the basis of a name, a partial name or extension, or even of a date.

When giving a filename or extension, just type in as many letters as you are sure about and leave the rest blank.

e_____ . w__ would find files such as **e**xpense.**w**ks, **e**stimate.**w**ps, **e**nglish.**w**db

You can narrow down the search by giving the date at which it was last used. You don't have to be specific here – the 'dates' range from *Today* to *Last Year.*

Note that File Organizer searches through every directory on a drive, but only one drive at a time.

Basic steps

1 Select **File Organizer** in the **WorksWizards** dialog box, or click [icon] the **Find File** button if you have added it to your toolbar.

2 Type in as much of the name as you can.

3 Select the **Drive**.

4 Set the **Date** range.

5 Click on **Start Search**.

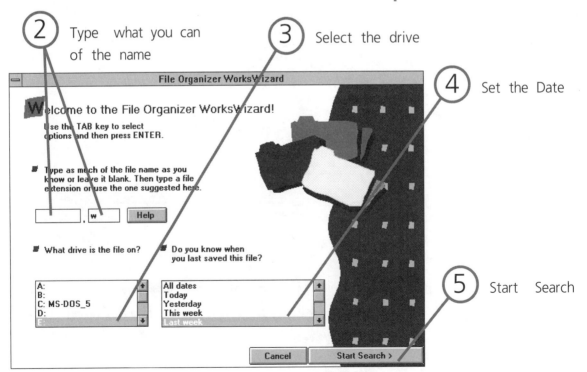

② Type what you can of the name

③ Select the drive

④ Set the Date

⑤ Start Search

6 If the search does not
find the file, click on
Redefine Search and try
again.

7 When your file turns up
in a list, select it.

8 Click a button on the
left to do what you
will with the file.

Tip

You can open files from
File Organizer, but if
you are not sure if you
have the right one, use
Preview to check it. This
is quicker than opening
them.

⑦ Select the file

⑧ Pick an operation

File Organizer WorksWizard

File names and dates last saved:

Scroll through the files and
select the one you're looking for.

Then you can redefine your
search or select from the
tasks below.

e:\msworks\bookfile\artpage.wps	07/06/94
e:\msworks\bookfile\tech.wcm	07/06/94
e:\msworks\bookfile\outline.wps	10/06/94
e:\msworks\bookfile\desktop.wps	10/06/94
e:\msworks\bookfile\plan.wdb	08/06/94
e:\msworks\bookfile\marks105.wps	11/06/94

Preview...

Open

Rename...

Move...

Copy...

Delete

Continue Search

Done   < Redefine Search

⑥ Try again?

Summary

❏ Works contains four main tools, **Word Processor**, **Spreadsheet**, **Database** and **Communications**, plus a set of smaller tools that can be called up from within the main ones.

❏ You can open any number of documents from the same or different tools at the same time, though your workspace may get crowded.

❏ All of Works' commands can be reached through the **menus**. These can be accessed from the keyboard by typing **[Alt]** followed by the underlined letter in the menu option name.

❏ The **Tools | Customize Toolbar** command lets you add buttons to, or remove them from, your toolbar. The **Find File** (File Organizer) is well worth adding.

❏ **Templates** offer a simple way to start new documents, as the basic structure and styles are already in place.

❏ **WorksWizards** mainly create customised databases, but there are also a Form Letter, a Letterhead and the File Organizer

❏ Documents from all the tools are saved by the same **File | Save** process. If wanted, they can be saved in different formats for transfer to other software.

❏ Existing documents are recalled with **File | Open**. Works can read in files that were created by other leading applications.

2 Getting help

The Help pages

Help is one thing you will never be short of in Works. In fact, you may feel that there is so much of it, you don't know where to start! You have:

The **Tutorial**, which covers many of the basic skills and concepts and is well worth spending a couple of hours on when you first start.

The **Help pages**, which contain much of the information from the manual and can be accessed through the **Contents** or the **Search** routes.

The **Cue Cards**, which take you step by step through many of the common processes.

When you are trying to find out how to do something, but aren't sure of the terminology, the best approach is through **Help Contents**. This will start with a list of the major areas of help on the current tool, and from here you can work through to the help page about a specific topic.

Basic steps

1 Open the **Help** menu and select **Contents**.

2 At the **Contents** list, click on the under-lined (green) text that best describes your interest.

3 At the second level list, click again on the likeliest heading. This may be followed by a third level list. Select again.

❑ This should take you to a Help page

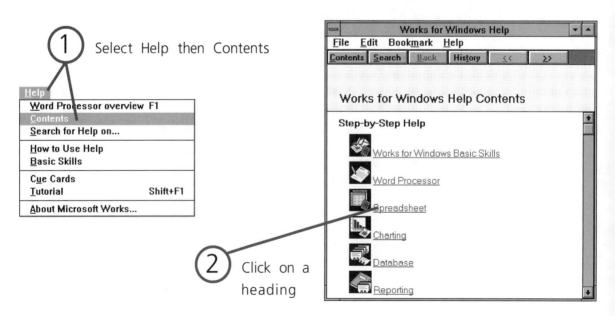

① Select Help then Contents

② Click on a heading

24

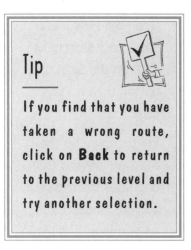

Tip

If you find that you have taken a wrong route, click on **Back** to return to the previous level and try another selection.

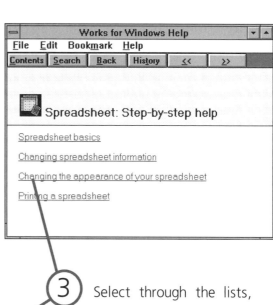

③ Select through the lists, focussing on your interest

Click here to step back to the previous list

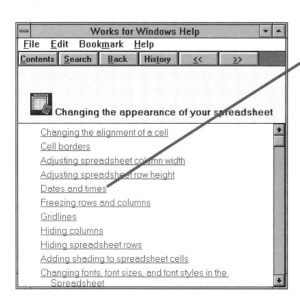

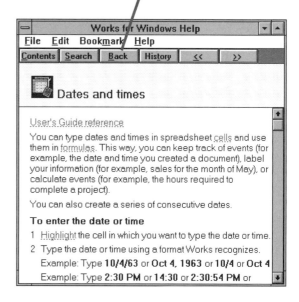

You will usually reach a Help page after 2 or 3 levels of selection.

Searching for Help

The Search route can be a quicker way to get to the right information, as long as you know what you are looking for. You don't have to be that exact, as the Help pages are cross-referenced. You can often get to the same page from several different start points, and once into the pages, you can easily switch between related topics.

Search can be reached from the Help menu, or from Help pages that you have opened via the Contents route.

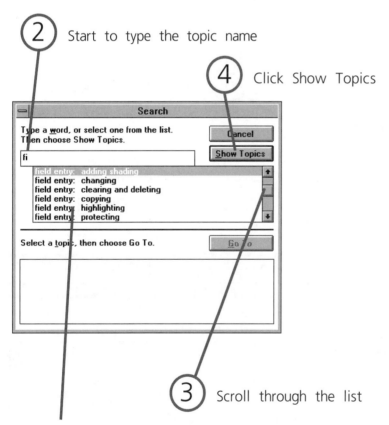

② Start to type the topic name

④ Click Show Topics

③ Scroll through the list

If you can't see anything promising, try a different key word for the topic

Basic steps

1 Open the **Help** menu and select **Search**, or click on the **Search** button on any Help page.

2 Start to type, in the top slot, a word that describes the topic you are interested in. As you type, the list in the **Show Topics** pane will adjust to show those that start with the same letters.

3 If necessary, scroll through the list until you can see a likely topic.

4 Highlight a topic and click the **Show Topics** button. The related pages will be listed in the **Go To** pane.

5 Highlight a topic in the new list and click **Go To** to open the Help page.

Moving round the Help pages

Contents and **Search** are the same as the Help menu options.

Back takes you to the previous Help page – not back to the Search screen.

History displays a list of the pages you have seen. Double click on one to go to it.

<< and **>>** move to other pages on the same topic.

Whether you reach your first Help page through Search or Contents, you will have the same options for moving from one page to another.

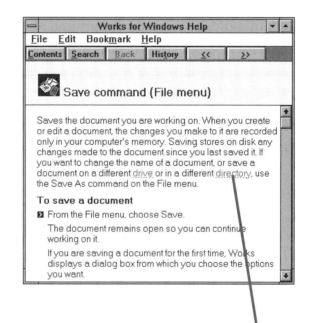

(5) Highlight a topic and click on Go To

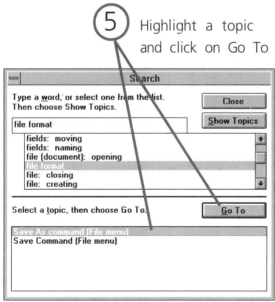

If a word has a dotted underline, clicking on it shows its Glossary entry. Anything with a solid underline will take you to another Help page.

Cue Cards

Cue Cards can be very useful when you are tackling a new job for the first time, as they will take you one step at a time through the process – rather as this book does. The catch to them is that they take up a fair chunk of screen space. There is not much you can do about this, as the cards are of fixed size, though you can shrink them down to icons if you want them out of the way for a moment.

1 Open the Help menu and select Cue Cards

2 The first card will introduce the concept and ask if you want to use the cards. Accept the offer, for now.

3 *Menu* cards carry [>] buttons. Click on these to select a task. *Steps* cards will often carry a [**Next >**] button. Click here when you have completed the steps.

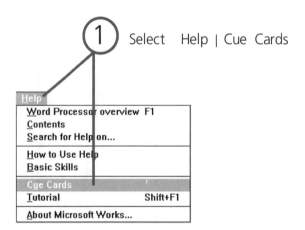

① Select   Help | Cue Cards

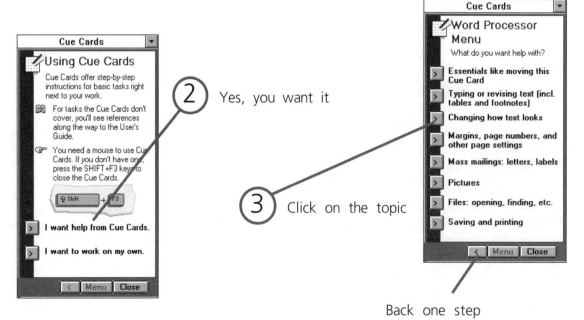

② Yes, you want it

③ Click on the topic

Back one step

28

Basic steps

Other Help

□ **Help with menus**

1 Open the menu with the mouse or an [Alt] letter combination.

2 Move the highlight to the option, either with the mouse or the arrow keys. **Do not click on it and set the command running!**

3 Press **[F1]** to open the Help page for the option.

In case the Help menu and Cue Cards are not enough, there are also two other ways of getting help. Both are context-sensitive – i.e. the pages they call up are directly related to the job in hand.

Press the **[F1]** key for help at any time. This is at its best if used on the menu options. (See left.)

All dialog boxes carry a [**Help**] button. Click on this for more information about the options in the box.

However you get into the Help system, once there you can move around freely between the pages.

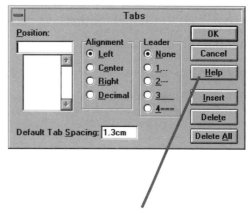

Help is never far away

Tip

Though you can press [F1] at any point when working on a document, it is often too general to be of much use. It is only with the menu options that it is specific and really useful.

Summary

❑ Works offers plenty of help to its users.

❑ **Help | Contents** takes you to lists of topics. You will usually have to work through two or three levels of lists to reach a page.

❑ **Help | Search** will take you more directly you a Help page, as long as you can describe what you want.

❑ When you are in the Help system, you can go back over previous pages or move around related topics.

❑ **Cue Cards** will take you step by step through a task, at the cost of obscuring part of the screen. This may be a price worth paying with a new and tricky job.

❑ You can get help on **menu** options by pressing **[F1]** when the option is highlighted.

❑ **Dialog boxes** carry a Help button to tell you more about the options in the box.

3 Working with text

Starting a new document

When you start a new document, there should be nothing in your main working area, apart from two straight lines.

The vertical, flashing, line is the **insertion point**. Wherever this is in the text, is where new text will be placed when you type or paste it in.

The horizontal line is the **end of document** marker.

The font name and size, alignment, margins and tabs settings shown on the toolbar and ruler will hold throughout the document – until you change them, though selected text and paragraphs within the document can have their own settings. If you want a significantly different appearance for your document, change the settings at the start.

Tip

When you first use the word processor, take a tour through the menus to get an idea of the range of facilities available to you.

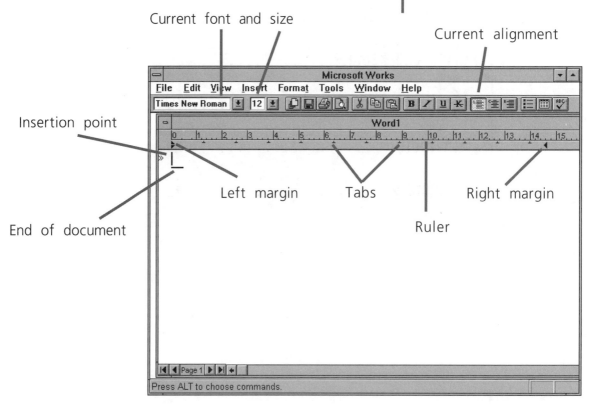

Current font and size

Current alignment

Insertion point

Left margin

Tabs

Right margin

End of document

Ruler

32

Instant edits

- ❑ If you want to go back in the text, move the insertion point with the arrow keys or by pointing and clicking the mouse.

- ❑ If you spot any errors, **[Backspace]** erases to the left of the insertion point, **[Delete]** erases to the right.

- ❑ If you have missed something out, move the insertion point back and type in the words. Existing text will shuffle up to make room for it.

Entering text

Don't think of the screen as a blank sheet of paper. You cannot start typing anywhere you like. The insertion point can only move where there is text or spaces. If you want to start over on the right, type spaces or tabs to push the insertion point across. If you want to start lower down on, press **[Enter]** to move the end of document marker down.

A word processor is not like a typewriter. When you reach the end of the line, just keep typing and let *wordwrap* take the text on to the next line for you. Do not press **[Enter]** until you reach the end of a paragraph.

The advantage of wordwrap is that you can change the width between the margins, and the text will still flow smoothly from one line to the next.

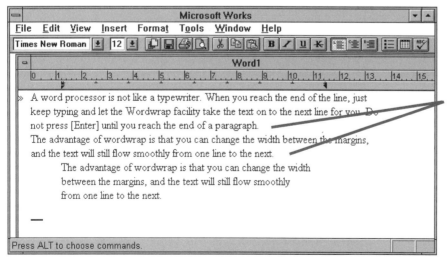

[Enter] at the end of paragraphs only

Selecting text

Text can be selected with the keys, but it is generally simplest to do it with the mouse. Once you have selected a block of text or a paragraph, you can:

● apply a font style or paragraph format – using the toolbar buttons or the Format menu. (See *Fonts and styles*, page 36 and *Paragraph formats*, page 46.)

● delete it – press [**Backspace**] or [**Delete**]

● move it – see the Steps

● get it into the Clipboard – see opposite

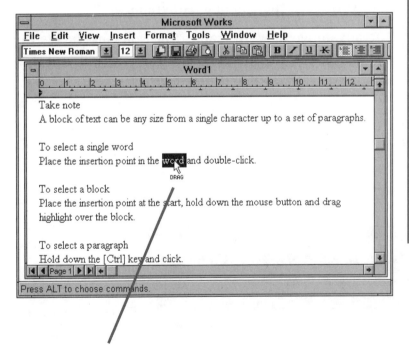

The DRAG will turn to MOVE or COPY as you drag it

❏ **To select a block:**

1 Place the insertion point at the start.

2 Hold down the mouse button and drag highlight to the end.

❏ **To select a word:**

1 Place the insertion point in the word and double-click.

❏ **To select a paragraph:**

1 Hold the [**Ctrl**] key.

2 Point and click any-where within the paragraph.

❏ **To select all the text:**

1 Open the **Edit** menu and choose **Select All**.

Take note

A block of text can be any size from one char-acter to a set of paragraphs or the whole document.

34

Basic steps

❏ **To drag and drop selected text:**

1 Point anywhere within the block.

2 Hold down the left button and drag the insertion point. You will see MOVE beside the pointer.

3 Release the button to drop the text in at the insertion point.

❏ **To copy selected text:**

1 Point anywhere within the block.

2 Hold down **[Ctrl]** while you drag the insertion point. You will see COPY beside the pointer.

3 Release the button to drop the text in at the insertion point.

Dragging and dropping text can only be done within a document – and can only be done easily when you are not moving the block very far. If you want to want to move a block over a distance, or from one document to another, you must use the **Edit** menu or toolbar buttons. Text can be cut or copied from your document into the Windows Clipboard, and then pasted wherever you want it.

● **Edit | Cut** removes the original text, storing a copy in the Clipboard;

● **Edit | Copy** copies the text into the Clipboard;

● **Edit | Paste** inserts a copy of whatever is in the Clipboard.

These are on the Edit menu of all Windows applications

This will select the whole text

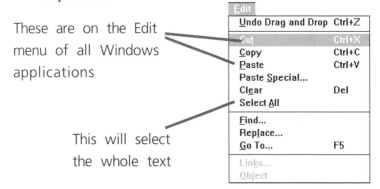

Take note

When you paste text from the Clipboard, it goes in after the insertion point or *replaces any text that is selected at the time.* Watch out for this, and check that nothing is highlighted, unless you do want to replace a block.

Fonts and styles

Font styles can be applied in two different ways.

● You can set them at the start, or at any point, to apply to everything you type afterwards – until you change them again.

● You can select a block, **anywhere in the middle of the text,** and apply a format to that block only.

All aspects of the appearance of text can be set through the **Format** menu, but if you are changing one feature only, it is often quicker to use the toolbar buttons or the keyboard shortcuts.

Basic steps

1 If you are formatting a block, select it first.

2 Open the **Format** menu and select **Font and Style...**

3 At the dialog box, start by selecting a **Font** from the list.

4 Change the **Size, Style** and other aspects next, checking the appearance of the text in the **Sample** pane.

5 Click **OK** when you are done.

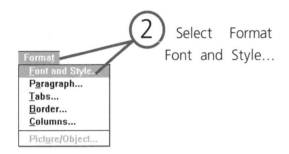

② Select Format Font and Style...

③ Set the Font

④ Check the Sample text

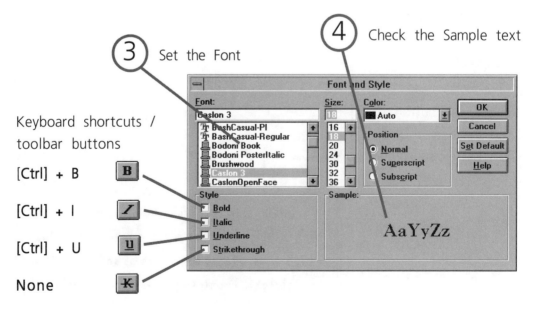

Keyboard shortcuts / toolbar buttons

[Ctrl] + B   **B**

[Ctrl] + I   **I**

[Ctrl] + U   **U**

None   **K**

Pull down the list to change
the Font from the toolbar

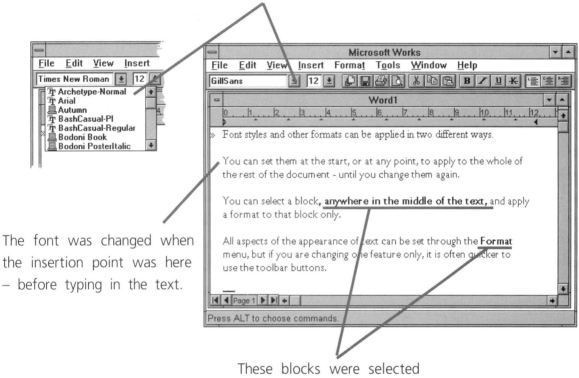

The font was changed when
the insertion point was here
– before typing in the text.

These blocks were selected
and then formatted.

Text sizes

9 point or less is for footnotes

12 point gives clear readable text

14 point works for sub-headings

18 point is good for titles

36 point makes a headline

Find and Replace

A simple **Find** will locate the next occurrence of a given word or phrase. You can use it to check documents for references to particular items, when you do not know if they are there or not. You can also use it to jump to a part of the document identified by a key word. The longer the document, the more useful this becomes.

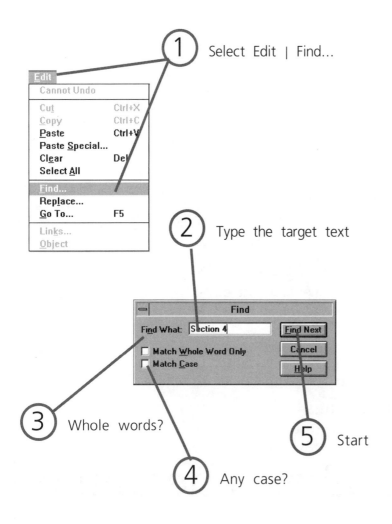

① Select Edit | Find...

② Type the target text

③ Whole words?

④ Any case?

⑤ Start

1 Open the **Edit** menu and select **Find**.

2 Type in the word or phrase you want to find.

3 If it might form part of a longer word, then check the **Match Whole Word Only** option.

4 If the pattern of capitals and lower case is important, check the **Match Case** option.

5 Click **Find Next** to start the search.

6 If the text is present, it will be found and highlighted. You can then either look for the next occurrence, or **Cancel** to return to the document – at the site of the found text.

Basic steps

1 Open the **Edit** menu and select **Replace**.

2 Type in the word or phrase you want to find, and the text that is to replace it.

3 Check the **Match Whole Word Only** and Match Case options if appropriate.

4 If you only want replace some of the occurrences, click **Find Next** to start, then click **Replace** when appropriate.

5 If you want a clean sweep, click **Replace All**

Tip

Before doing a Replace All on a short word, check both the Match options. There is a chance the word will occur *inside* another.

Find and Replace will find the given text and replace it with a new phrase. it is said that some unscrupulous authors use this to make new books from old. A quick Replace on the names of the key characters and of the places, and you have a fresh novel! It is more commonly used as a time-saver. If you had a long name, such as Butterworth-Heinemann, that needed to be written several times in a document, you could instead type an abbreviation, B-H, and later use Replace to swap the full name back in.

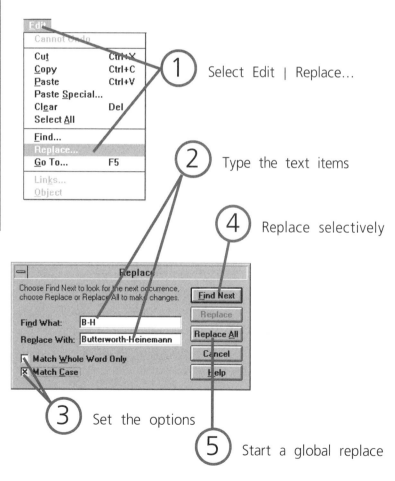

① Select Edit | Replace...

② Type the text items

④ Replace selectively

③ Set the options

⑤ Start a global replace

Spell checks

Even the best spellers need these! You may not make spelling mistakes, but is your typing perfect?

The spelling checker works from a dictionary of over 100,000 words. It's a good number, but there will be some words that you use that are not present. Specialised terms and names of people and places are the most likely omissions. To cope with these, there is a user dictionary, to which you can add your own selection of words. Once added, they will be included in the checks next time around.

The check can be run over a single, selected word, over a highlighted block, or throughout the doument.

Basic steps

1 If you only want to check one word, or a block, select it first.

2 Open the **Tools** menu and select **Spelling**, or click

3 When an unknown word is found you will be offered several ways to deal with it. Edit it, if you can see the error, or click a button.

2 Select Tools | Spelling

Tools
Dial This Number
Spelling...
Thesaurus...
Hyphenation...
Word Count
Envelopes and Labels...
Paginate Now   F9
Customize Toolbar...
Options...

3 Edit or click an option

It's OK, leave it...

... every time you see it

Add the word to your personal dictionary

Spelling

Not in Dictionary: Butterworth

Change To: Butterworth

Suggestions: No suggestions.

Ignore   Ignore All
Change   Change All
Add   Cancel
Suggest   Help

☐ Skip capitalized words
☐ Always Suggest

Useful where there are a lot of names

Brings up a list, putting the most likely into the **Change To** slot, and enabling the **Change** buttons.

Basic steps

1 Select the word you would like to replace.

2 Open the **Tools** menu and select **Thesaurus** or click 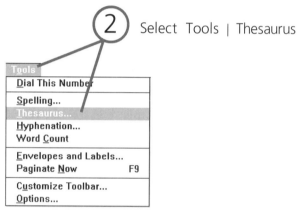 if you have added it to your toolbar.

3 If the word can have several **Meanings**, select the closest from the list on the left.

4 Select a word from the **Synonyms** list on the right.

5 Click **Change** to replace the word with the current synonym.

Stuck for *le mot juste*? Let the Thesaurus suggest (offer, propound, submit, advise, propose) a better (preferred, improved, superior) word. With a bank of just under 200,000 words to draw from, it can generally come up with something suitable (apropos, pertinent, relevant, applicable, germane).

② Select Tools | Thesaurus

③ Pick the closest meaning

④ Pick a synonym

⑤ Click Change

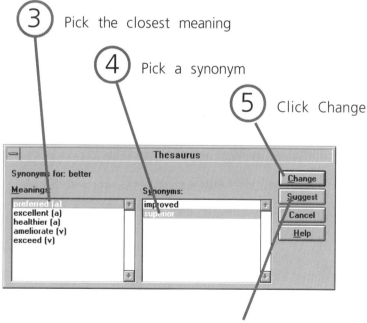

More alternatives

Tip

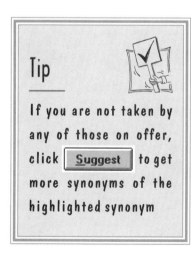

If you are not taken by any of those on offer, click **Suggest** to get more synonyms of the highlighted synonym

Summary

❏ When you start a new document, there are default settings for fonts and formats already in place. Change these at the start if you want a different appearance.

❏ The **Insertion Point** shows where text will appear when you type. Move it with the arrow keys or the mouse if you want to go back into your text to edit it.

❏ Corrections can be made as you type by pressing **[Backspace]**, or left for tidying up later.

❏ A **selected** block of text can be formatted, deleted or moved to a new position.

❏ The Clipboard's **Edit Cut** and **Paste** facilities allow you to copy and move text between pages and between documents.

❏ **Find** will search documents for particular words, and can be used to jump to the location of a word.

❏ **Replace** lets you type in abbreviations, and replace them all at the end ina single operation.

❏ The **Spelling** checker is an invaluable aid for spotting mistypes, as well as spelling errors.

❏ The **Thesaurus** can help you to find the most appropriate words to express your meaning.

4 Page layout

Page setup

Before you get too far into typing the text, you should check that the basic layout of the page is right. Use the **Page Setup** routine to set the paper size, orientation and margins. And check the effect of these settings with **Print Preview** or by switching to **Page Layout** view.

Basic steps

1 Open the **File** menu and select Page Setup...

2 Adjust the **Margins** to suit.

3 Open the **Source, Size and Orientation** panel. Check the **Paper size**. Change the **Orientation** to *Landscape* if you want to print sideways.

① Select File | Page Setup...

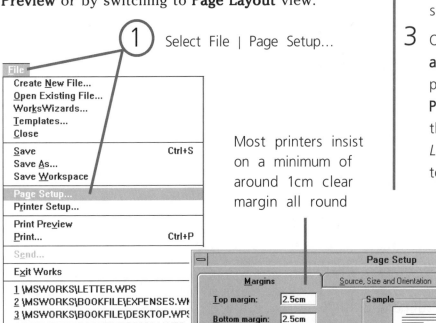

Most printers insist on a minimum of around 1cm clear margin all round

Header and Footer margins must be less than Top and Bottom margins

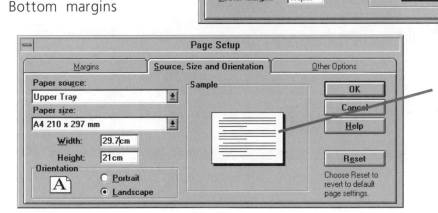

The Sample gives a rough idea of how a page will look.

Basic steps

1 Open the **File** menu
and select **Print Pre-
view..** or click on the
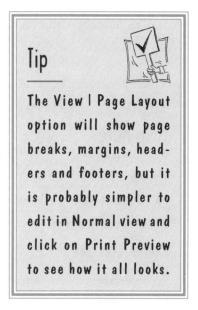 button.

2 If you want to take a
closer look, don't use
the **Zoom In** button.
Point the magnifying
glass and click – it
gets you to the right
place. Click again to
get even closer, and a
third time to switch
back to the full page.

3 **Cancel** to return
to editing.

See also *Printing*, page 58.

Tip

**The View | Page Layout
option will show page
breaks, margins, head-
ers and footers, but it
is probably simpler to
edit in Normal view and
click on Print Preview
to see how it all looks.**

Print Preview

There's no point in waiting until the document is finished
before you check how it will look when printed. Use Print
Preview whenever you are making adjustments to the
layout or the fonts.

(1) Select File | Print Preview...

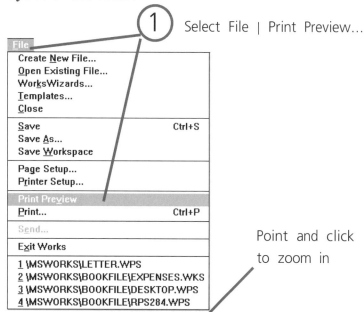

Point and click
to zoom in

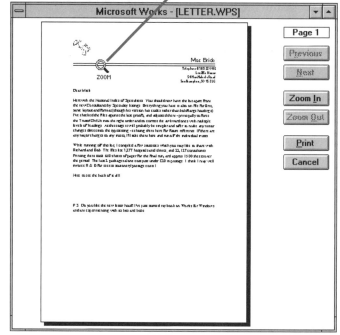

Paragraph formats

As with font styles, paragraph formats can apply to:

● all subsequent text, if the insertion point is at the end of the document when the format is set, or

● selected paragraphs – i.e. a highlighted set, or the one containing the insertion point.

All aspects of formatting are covered by the **Format | Paragraphs** command. There are also toolbar buttons to handle alignments – and spacing if you include them.

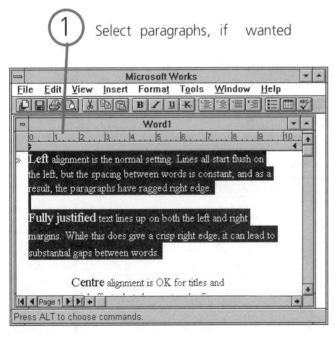

① Select paragraphs, if wanted

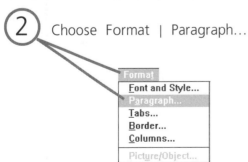

② Choose Format | Paragraph...

Basic steps

1 Select the paragraphs you want to format, unless you are setting defaults for all new text.

2 Open the **Format** menu and select **Paragraph...**

3 At the Paragraph dialog box, turn to the **Quick Formats** page, to use a preset design, or to either **Indents and Alignment** or **Breaks and Spacing** to specify settings.

4 Click **OK** or press **[Enter]** when you have done setting options.

Take note

The Justified button can be added to the toolbar with the Customize Toolbar routine.

Quick formats

Use these if you want the simple solution. There are five standard formats, one of which should do the job. The Sample pane gives you a good idea of how the layout will look.

Pick a Style

Check the sample

Click to open the other panels

Click OK

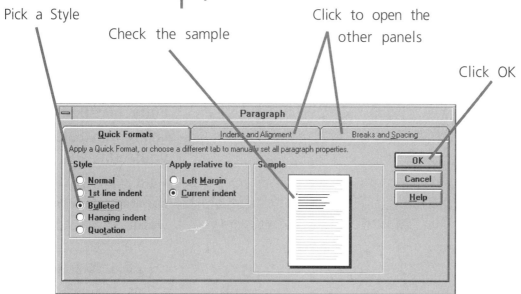

Normal text has all its lines aligned to the left.

If you are using this style, you should leave a space between paragraphs, so they don't all run into one solid mass.

    1st line indent pushes in the first line only, emphasising the start of a new paragraph.

- **Bulleted** text has all lines indented, with a blob by the first.
- Use it for lists or wherever you want to make a set of short, sharp points.

Hanging indent pushes in all lines except for the first. You might use it where the first word is a term that is defined by the following text.

Quotation indents all lines from both left and right, and puts a line space above and below the paragraph.

Indents and Alignment

The second panel of the Paragraphs box gives you control over indents and alignments. Most of its functions can be done almost as well from toolbar buttons, though it is only in the box that you can set indents really accurately.

● **Bullets** can be added from the toolbar button, but the only way to remove them is by turning them off in this panel.

Indents are easier to set with the Ruler. See opposite

Select the alignment

Check it

Click OK

Paragraph

| Quick Formats | Indents and Alignment | Breaks and Spacing |

Set indentation and alignment, or choose the Quick Formats tab for preset options.

Indents
Left: `0.6cm`
Right: `0cm`
First Line: `-0.6cm`

☒ Bulleted

Alignment
◉ Left
○ Center
○ Right
○ Justified

Sample

OK
Cancel
Help

Click here to add or remove bullets.

Alignment

Left ▤ alignment is the normal setting. Lines start flush on the left, but as the spacing between words is constant, the paragraphs have ragged right edge.

Fully justified ▤ text aligns with both margins. While this gives a crisp right edge, it can lead to substantial gaps between words.

Centre ▤ alignment is OK for titles and special effects, but does not make for easy reading.

Right ▤ alignment is used for addresses and other headings and for dates.

Indents

1 If the **Ruler** is not
visible, open the **View**
menu and click on
Ruler.

❏ **To set the Right
indent:**

Point anywhere on the
right triangle and drag
it into position.

❏ **To set the Left indent:**

Point at the *lower* left
triangle and drag.

❏ **To set the First line
indent:**

Point at the *upper* left
triangle and drag.

The width of lines of text can be controlled by both
Margins and Indents.

● **Margins** are printer settings and controlled by the
Page Setup routines. (See page 44.).

● **Indents** push the text in further from the margins,
and are used to pick out paragraphs, for emphasis.

> Left and Right indents set the distance of all
> lines from the relevant margins. This para-
> graph has a left indent of 1.5cm, and a right
> indent of 1cm.

First line indent sets the difference between the first and
later lines. It can be negative - left of the left
indent - to create a **hanging indent**, as here.

Indents can be set most accurately by typing values into
the **Indents and Alignments** page of the **Paragraph** dialog
box, but much of the time it is simpler to use the indent
marker triangles on the ruler.

Tip

**Make sure the
margins are right
before fiddling
with the indents.**

First line indent   Left indent   Right indent

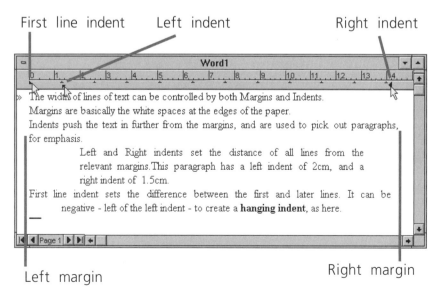

Left margin   Right margin

Breaks and Spacing

Breaks refers to what happens to paragraphs at the bottom of a page. Works will normally print as many lines as fit neatly on the page – not worrying about awkward breaks in mid-paragraph. If you want to ensure that a paragraph stays intact, even though it may mean a large gap at the bottom of a page, then set the **Don't break paragraph** option for it.

Spacing

For most purposes, it is enough to be able to switch between single-line spacing and double-spacing. Double-spacing can be used for emphasis, though **bold**, *italics* or larger text will do that better. It is best kept for those times when you want to leave space between lines for people to write notes or corrections.

Single ▣ and double space ▣ buttons can be added to the toolbar. You will find them in the Format set in the Customize Toolbar dialog box.

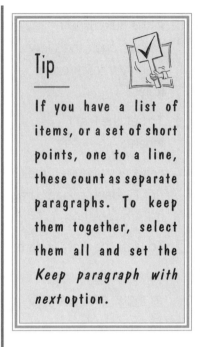

Tip

If you have a list of items, or a set of short points, one to a line, these count as separate paragraphs. To keep them together, select them all and set the *Keep paragraph with next* option.

Press [Enter] after typing a value or click OK to exit

Just type the number to set spacing in lines.

Add mm to set it in millimetres.

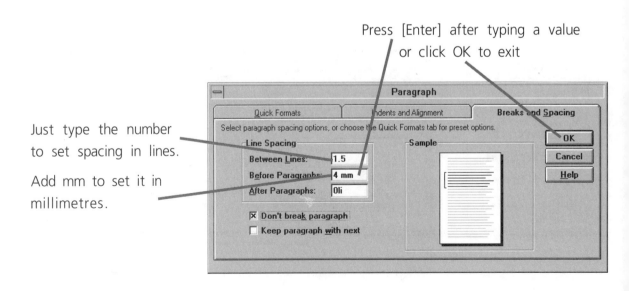

Borders and lines

If you want to place lines anywhere around a block of text, use Format | Borders..

A line below a paragraph can mark off the end of a section.

> Lines on either side can help to emphasise a block of text.

Lines all round the outside create a solid box. This can work well around the title on the front page of a report.

To make a box narrower, or pull in the side lines, select the paragraph and drag the indent markers inwards.

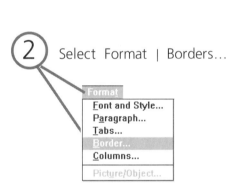

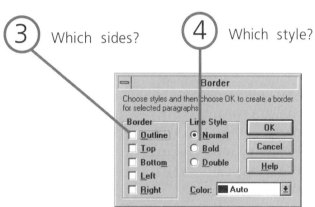

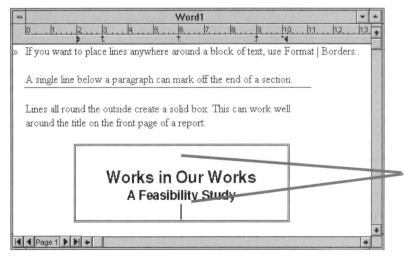

To make a space above or below the text, include blank lines when you select the paragraph.

Setting tabs

Tab setting is not difficult, but it can get fiddly if you want anything other than plain left tabs. Placing centre, right and decimal tabs can be made simpler by bringing their buttons (from the Format set) onto the toolbar.

You must use the Tabs dialog box to:

● fine-tune their positions, as they do not move smoothly along the ruler

● add Leader dots or lines

● delete tabs

⬚ Left tabs are for general use;

⬚ Right tabs are used for simple numbers, such as index or contents entries;

Left Tab	Right Tab
I	I
Fields, green	108
Fields, in records	20
Files, opening	142
Files, saving	7

⬚ Centre tabs give much the same effect as Centre alignment

⬚ Decimal tabs line up money values, to the right, by their decimal points.

Decimal
|
Widgets, large leather ----------------- 17.99
Widgets, small furry ---------------------- 1.295
Widgets, gold-plated---------------3,587.50

1 Select the block in which you want tabs.

2 If you have added the tabs buttons, click on the type you want.

3 Click on the Ruler to place a tab, dragging it into position, if necessary.

4 To change the type of tab, adjust its position accurately, or add leader dots, open the **Format** menu and select **Tabs....**

5 Pick the tab and adjust as necessary.

6 Click **Insert** to store the settings.

7 Return to 4 to adjust another tab.

8 Click **OK** when all are done.

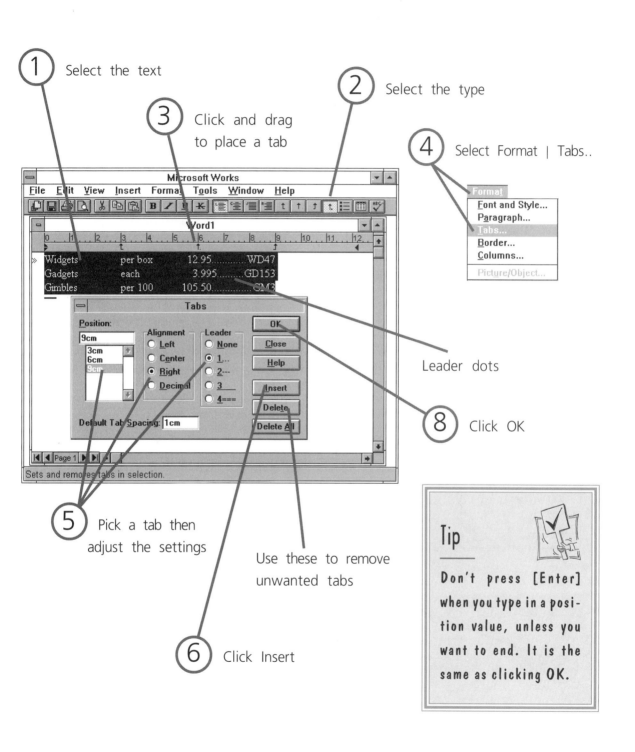

1 Select the text

2 Select the type

3 Click and drag to place a tab

4 Select Format | Tabs..

Leader dots

8 Click OK

5 Pick a tab then adjust the settings

Use these to remove unwanted tabs

6 Click Insert

Tip

Don't press [Enter] when you type in a position value, unless you want to end. It is the same as clicking OK.

Headers and footers

Headers and footers, if defined, will appear at the top and bottom of every page. They can contain plain text and special codes. The text might be a report title, chapter heading or author, and the codes can be used to give the date or the page number, and to set the alignment.

All codes start with an ampersand (&). The main ones are:

&d   current date

&p   page number

&l   left align following text

&r   right align following text

&c   centre align following text

Basic steps

1 Open the **View** menu and select **Headers and Footers...**

2 Type in the text and codes that you want to appear at the top and bottom of each page.

3 If you don't want them on the first (title?) page, check the **No header(footer) on 1st page** options

4 Click **OK**.

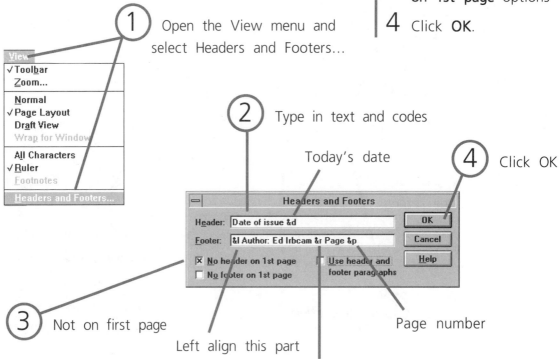

① Open the View menu and select Headers and Footers...

View
√ Tool**b**ar
Zoom...

Normal
√ Page **L**ayout
Dr**a**ft View
Wra**p** for Window

A**l**l Characters
√ **R**uler
Footnotes

Headers and Footers...

② Type in text and codes

Today's date

④ Click OK

Headers and Footers

H**e**ader: | Date of issue &d | **OK**

Footer: | &l Author: Ed Irbcam &r Page &p | **Cancel**

☒ **N**o header on 1st page   ☐ **U**se header and footer parag**r**aphs   **Help**
☐ N**o** footer on 1st page

③ Not on first page

Left align this part

Page number

Right align from here

Headers and footers are invisible in the Normal view, as they are only really intended for enhancing the print out.

To see them, use either:

File | Print Preview for a clear look at the whole page, or

View | Page Layout so that you can see them and edit your text.

Text is normally centred

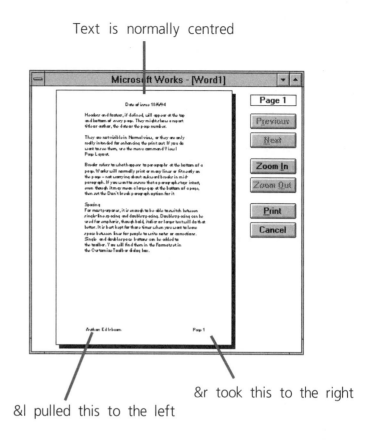

&l pulled this to the left

&r took this to the right

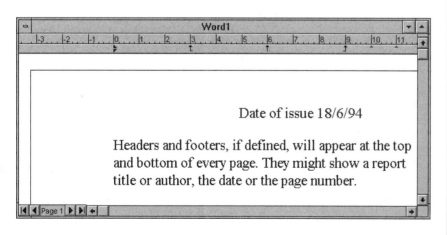

Date of issue 18/6/94

Headers and footers, if defined, will appear at the top and bottom of every page. They might show a report title or author, the date or the page number.

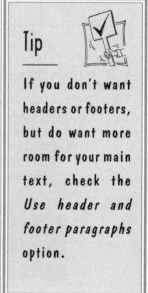

Tip

If you don't want headers or footers, but do want more room for your main text, check the *Use header and footer paragraphs* option.

Columns

Use a multiple column layout where you want to have a number of separate stories on a page, or where a report is broken down into a set of distinct, headed paragraphs, perhaps interspersed with graphics.

Short paragraphs, that cover only a couple of lines across the full width of the page, will take 6 or 8 lines in columns. These solid blocks of text look more balanced and are easier to read.

You would normally want two or three columns on an A4 page – with four or more, the columns are too narrow, unless you are using a very small point size. Anything less than three or four words to a line looks far too scrappy.

Basic steps

1 Open the **Format** menu and select **Columns...**

2 At the dialog box, set the **Number of columns** and the **Space between** them.

3 Check **Lines between** if you want them. These will not be visible during editing, but are appl;ied at print time.

4 Click **OK**.

5 Start typing and leave Works to flow the text into the columns.

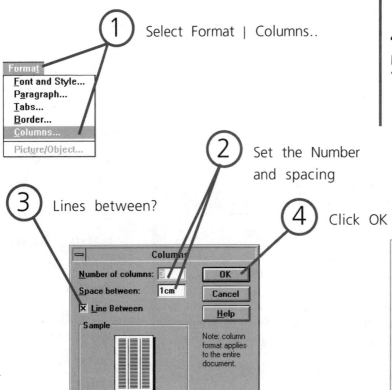

Select Format | Columns..

Set the Number and spacing

Lines between?

Click OK

Take note

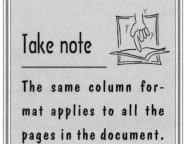

The same column format applies to all the pages in the document.

Text can only be written inside the columns, but if you want headlines across the page, insert Word Art text. (See *Word Art.*)

Short items can be picked out by dropping a border round them. You cannot do easily with a whole page format.

Short paragraphs work better in columns

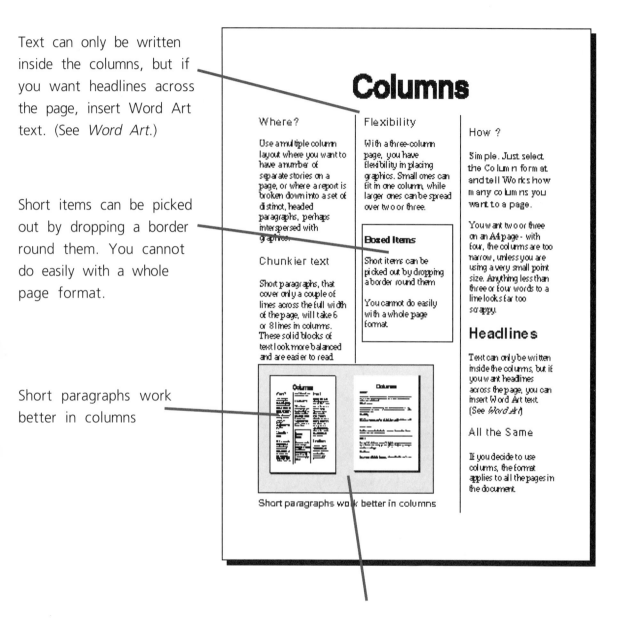

Columns

Where?

Use a multiple column layout where you want to have a number of separate stories on a page, or where a report is broken down into a set of distinct, headed paragraphs, perhaps interspersed with graphics.

Chunkier text

Short paragraphs, that cover only a couple of lines across the full width of the page, will take 6 or 8 lines in columns. These solid blocks of text look more balanced and are easier to read.

Flexibility

With a three-column page, you have flexibility in placing graphics. Small ones can fit in one column, while larger ones can be spread over two or three.

Boxed Items

Short items can be picked out by dropping a border round them

You cannot do easily with a whole page format.

How ?

Simple. Just select the Column format and tell Works how many columns you want to a page.

You want two or three on an A4 page - with four, the columns are too narrow, unless you are using a very small point size. Anything less than three or four words to a line looks far too scrappy.

Headlines

Text can only be written inside the columns, but if you want headlines across the page, you can insert Word Art text. (See *Word Art*)

All the Same

If you decide to use columns, the format applies to all the pages in the document.

Short paragraphs work better in columns

With a three-column page, you have flexibility in placing graphics. Small ones can fit in one column, while larger ones can be spread over two or three.

Printing

Page Layout view and the Print Preview facility give you a good idea of how the document will appear, but you can never be entirely sure until you see the printed copy. Some fonts do not come out quite the same on paper as on screen; grey shades become dot patterns; colours are never quite the same. If you have a long document, it is often worth printing a couple of sample pages, and checking those, before committing the whole lot to paper.

Basic steps

1 Open the **File** menu and select **Print** or click 🖨 on the toolbar.

2 Set the **Number of Copies**.

3 Set the **Page Range**, specifying **Start** and **End** pages, or **All**.

4 Click **OK**

(1) Select File | Print..

File

Create **N**ew File...	
Open Existing File...	
Wor**k**sWizards...	
Templates...	
Close	
Save	Ctrl+S
Save **A**s...	
Save **W**orkspace	
Pa**g**e Setup...	
Pr**i**nter Setup...	
Print Pre**v**iew	
Print...	Ctrl+P
S**e**nd...	
E**x**it Works	
1 \MSWORKS\BOOKFILE\REPLACE.WPS	
2 \MSWORKS\BOOKFIL	
3 \MSWORKS\BOOKFIL	
4 \MSWORKS\BOOKFIL	

(2) How many copies?

(3) Which pages?

(4) Click OK

Print

Printer: Okidata OL-400 on LPT1:

Number of **C**opies: [1]

Print Range
- ○ **A**ll
- ● **P**ages
- **F**rom: [1] **T**o: [7]

What to print
- ● **M**ain Document
- ○ **E**nvelope

- ☐ Pr**i**nt merge
- ☐ **D**raft quality printing

OK
Preview
Test
Cancel
Help

Preview if you want to check first

Tip

Check the Draft quality option when you are just doing a quick printout for your own use. Make sure it is off when printing the final copy.

Basic steps

1 Open the **File** menu
   and select **Printer
   Setup...**

2 If you are switching to
   another printer, select
   it from the list.

3 If you want to adjust
   the print settings, click
   Setup...

4 Set the **Paper** details
   and the **Orientation**
   as required.

5 If you want to adjust
   the blackness of the
   print, click **Options...**
   and set the **Intensity
   Control**.

Dithering handles grey
shades. Select Coarse for
higher-resolution printers;
Fine for those less than
200 dots per inch

Improves print speed and
quality where there is
mixed text and graphics

Printer setup

Works runs through Windows, and the Printer Setup
routines that you will have done there, will be in place for
your Works printing. As a result, you will probably find
that you only have to bother with this on rare occasions.
Use Setup when you want to switch to a second printer,
or print sideways, or adjust the quality of the print.

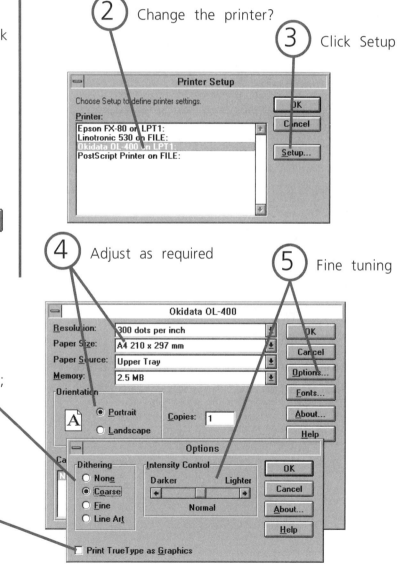

(2) Change the printer?

(3) Click Setup

Printer Setup
Choose Setup to define printer settings.
Printer:
Epson FX-80 on LPT1:
Linotronic 530 on FILE:
Okidata OL-400 on LPT1:
PostScript Printer on FILE:

OK
Cancel
Setup...

(4) Adjust as required

(5) Fine tuning

Okidata OL-400
Resolution: 300 dots per inch
Paper Size: A4 210 x 297 mm
Paper Source: Upper Tray
Memory: 2.5 MB
Orientation
A ● Portrait   Copies: 1
   ○ Landscape

OK
Cancel
Options...
Fonts...
About...
Help

Options
Dithering   Intensity Control
○ None   Darker   Lighter
● Coarse
○ Fine   Normal
○ Line Art

□ Print TrueType as Graphics

OK
Cancel
About...
Help

Summary

- ❏ Use the **Page Setup** routines to set the paper size, orientation and margins.

- ❏ The **Format | Paragraph** dialog box has a set of **Quick Formats** that will suit many purposes.

- ❏ **Indents, Alignment** and **Tabs** can be set from the ruler or toolbar buttons, though you may have to use the dialog boxes to get fine control.

- ❏ You can control how paragraphs behave at page **Breaks** and set the **Spacing** between lines and between paragraphs.

- ❏ **Borders** can be added to any or all of the edges of a selected block of text.

- ❏ **Tabs** are easily set via the Ruler, but for more accurate positioning you should use the **Format | Tabs** dialog box.

- ❏ **Headers** and **Footers** can be added if wanted. There are special codes to control alignment, page numbers and dates.

- ❏ Multiple **columns** offer a number of advantages for newsletters and certain types of reports.

- ❏ Check the settings before printing. If required, you can adjust them in the Print Setup dialog box.

5 Working with numbers

Cells and contents

A spreadsheet is a grid of cells into which text, numbers and formulae can be written. With the Works spreadsheet, you also have control of fonts, lines and background patterns to enhance the appearance, so that, for example, the spreadsheet that calculates the blls can also produce professional-looking invoices. Where the spreadsheet is being used to analyse cash flows, departmental budgets or other sets of values that change over time or category, the easy chart-drawing routines can make the patterns of change more visible.

Two layers

With a word processor document, what you see is what you get. Spreadsheets are different. The text, numbers and formulae that are held in the cells are not necessarily what you see on screen. With formulae, the results are displayed; text items that are longer than the width of the cell will be clipped short if there is something in the cell to the right; numbers will appear as a set of # if they are too large to fit in a cell.

Entering and editing data

Entering data into a spreadsheet is significantly different from entering it into a word processor. Everything goes in through the Formula line, where the system checks it to see if it is a piece of text, a number or a formula – for these are each treated differently. The Formula line is linked to the current cell. It displays whatever is in the cell at the moment, and anything entered into the formula line is transferred to the cell.

❑ **To enter data:**

1 Point at the target cell and click on it to make it current.

2 Start to type. The characters will appear in the formula line.

3 Use the **[Left]** / **[Right]** arrow keys to move along the line; **[Backspace]** or **[Delete]** to erase errors.

4 Click ☑ or press **[Enter]** when you have done. The display version of the data will appear in the cell.

❑ **To edit cell contents:**

1 Make the target cell current.

2 Click in the Formula line, or press **[F2]** to start editing.

3 Click ☑ or press **[Enter]** to accept the changes. Click ☒ or press **[Escape]** to abandon

Jargon

Current cell – the last one you clicked with the mouse. It is marked by double-line borders.

Cell reference – a Column letter/Row number combination that identifies a cell. In the diagram, the current cell is C12 (Column C, Row 12).

Range - a set of cells, which may be one or more full rows or columns, or a block somewhere in the middle of the sheet.

Formula line – the slot at the top. Its contents are transferred to the current cell when you press **[Enter]**. All data is entered into cells through this line.

Wide text will flow over into empty cells.

Column letters

Formula line

Fonts and Formats

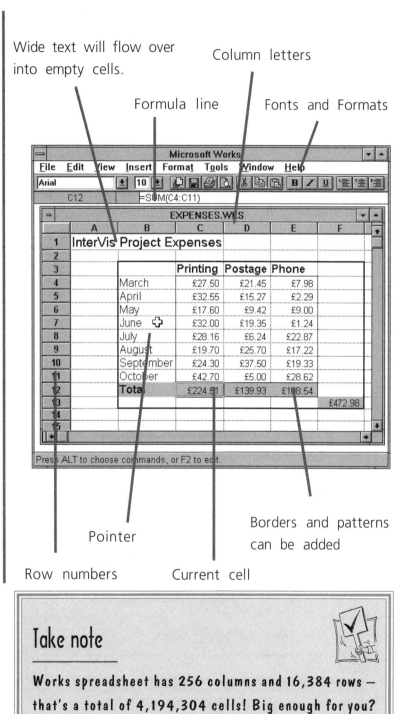

Pointer

Row numbers

Current cell

Borders and patterns can be added

Current cell

Take note

Works spreadsheet has **256 columns** and **16,384 rows** – that's a total of **4,194,304 cells!** Big enough for you?

63

Selecting cells and ranges

Once you have selected a cell, or a range of cells, you can:

- apply a font style or alignment;
- add a border to some or all of its edges;
- erase its contents;
- use its references in a formula.
- move it to another position;

If you have to type a range reference, it is made up of the cell references of the top left and bottom right corners. Most of the time you will be able to get the references by selecting the range with the mouse.

❏ **To select a block:**

1 Point to the top left cell (or any corner).

2 Hold down the mouse button and drag the highlight over the block.

❏ **To select a set of rows:**

1 Point to the row number at the top or bottom of the set.

2 Drag up or down over the numbers to highlight the rows you want.

① Start here

Block references shown here

② Drag to the opposite corner

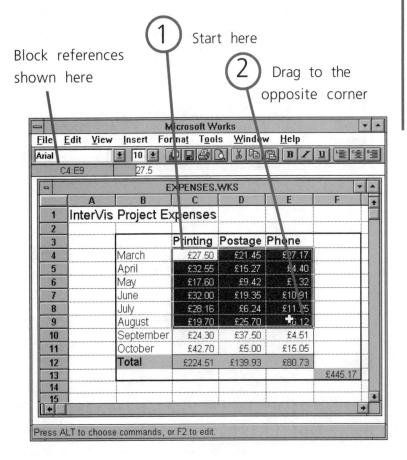

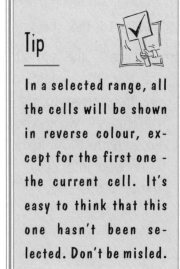

Tip

In a selected range, all the cells will be shown in reverse colour, except for the first one - the current cell. It's easy to think that this one hasn't been selected. Don't be misled.

❏ **To select a set of columns:**

1 Point to the column letter at one end of the set.

2 Drag across the top of the columns to include the ones you want.

❏ **To select all cells:**

1 Click on the top left corner, where the row and column headers meet,

or

open the **Edit** menu and choose **Select All**.

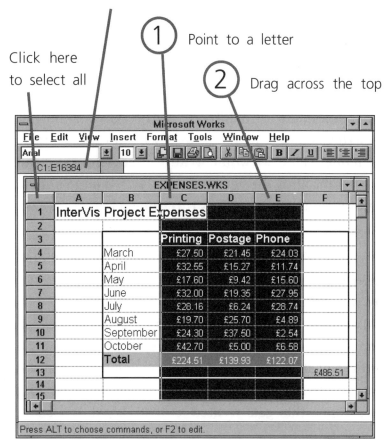

① Point to a letter

② Drag across the top

Click here to select all

① Open the Edit menu and choose Select All

These select the Row or Column of the current cell – clicking is quicker!

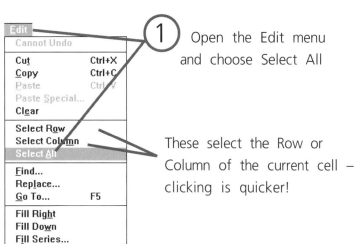

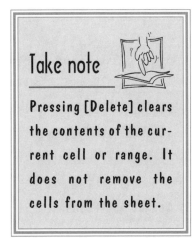

Take note

Pressing [Delete] clears the contents of the current cell or range. It does not remove the cells from the sheet.

Fonts and formats

Setting font types, styles and sizes for text is exactly the same here as it is in the word processor. Just select the block to be restyled and click a toolbar button or use the **Format | Font and Style** dialog box.

Number formats are a different matter. The way in which we write a number depends upon what it represents. If it is a money value, we would write a £ sign before and show two figures after the decimal point; with a large number, we would put commas every three digits to make it easier to read; if it is a percent, we place a % sign after it.

Works knows about all this. It can display numbers in different formats, and it can understand numbers that are written in different formats. Type in £12,345.67 and it will realise that the underlying number is 12345.67, and also that you want to display it as currency. Type in 50% and it will store it as 0.5, while showing 50% on screen. Type in 081-123 4567 and it will not be fooled into thinking its a sum – this gets treated as text. Try it and see for yourself.

Basic steps

1 Select the range of cells to be formatted.

2 Open the **Format** menu and select **Number...**

3 Select a **Format** from the panel on the left.

4 Set the number of decimal places.

5 With *Currency* values, you may want to use the **Negative numbers in red** option.

6 Check the Sample and adjust the options as required.

7 Click **OK**.

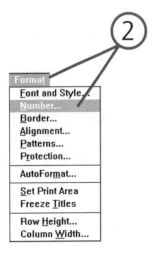

② Open the Format menu and select Number...

Take note

The Currency button is part of the standard toolbar set. Buttons can be added for Comma and Percent.

General is the default – numbers appear as they were written.

Currency 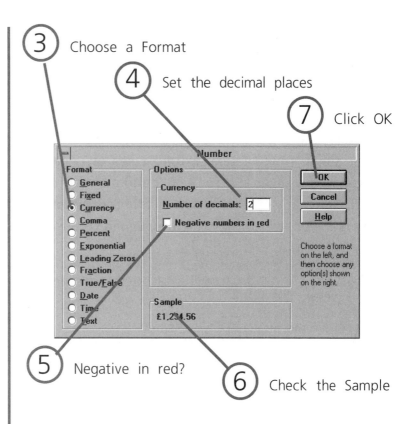 places a £ at the front, commas every 3 digits.

Commas places a comma every 3 digits.

Percent multiplies the value by 100 and adds the % sign at the end.

Exponential is used for very large or very small numbers.

Text treats the digits as text, not as a value.

③ Choose a Format

④ Set the decimal places

⑦ Click OK

Number

Format
- ○ General
- ○ Fixed
- ● Currency
- ○ Comma
- ○ Percent
- ○ Exponential
- ○ Leading Zeros
- ○ Fraction
- ○ True/False
- ○ Date
- ○ Time
- ○ Text

Options

Currency

Number of decimals: 2

☐ Negative numbers in red

Sample
£1,234.56

OK
Cancel
Help

Choose a format on the left, and then choose any option(s) shown on the right.

⑤ Negative in red?

⑥ Check the Sample

A small selection of the number formats that Works can handle. The number of decimal places can be set in any format. With Currency and Comma formats, you can have negative numbers shown in red.

	A	B	C	D	E	F
	FORMATS.WKS					
1	General	Currency	Comma, 1DP	Percent, 0DP	Exponent	Text
2	1	£1.00	1.0	100%	1.00E+00	1
3	1.2	£1.20	1.2	120%	1.20E+00	1.2
4	1.2345	£1.23	1.2	123%	1.23E+00	1.2345
5	1234	£1,234.00	1,234.0	123400%	1.23E+03	1234
6	1234567	£1,234,567.00	1,234,567.0	123456700%	1.23E+06	1234567
7	0.123	£0.12	0.1	12%	1.23E-01	0.123
8	-12.3	-£12.30	-12.3	-1230%	-1.23E+01	-12.3
9	1235792.258	£1,235,792.26	1,235,792.3	123579226%	1.24E+06	=SUM(F2:F8)
10						

There are formulae at the bottom of each colum to add up the total. Look what happens with the Text 'numbers'.

Alignment

There are more alignment options in the Spreadsheet than in the Word Processor. **Left**, **Right** and **Centre** alternatives, which can be used to align text within cells, are available on the toolbar ⊟ ⊟ ⊟ . The **Format** | **Alignment** dialog box also has **Fill** and **Centre**, which align a single item of text within a set of cells, and **General**, which aligns text to the left and numbers to the right. This works well, though the headings of columns of numbers look better if they too are aligned to the right.

1 Select the range of cells to be aligned.

2 Open the **Format** menu and select **Alignment...**

3 Select an **Alignment** option.

4 If you want to adjust the **Vertical** position of the text within the cell, set an option.

5 Click **OK**.

① Select the block

② Open the Format menu and select Number...

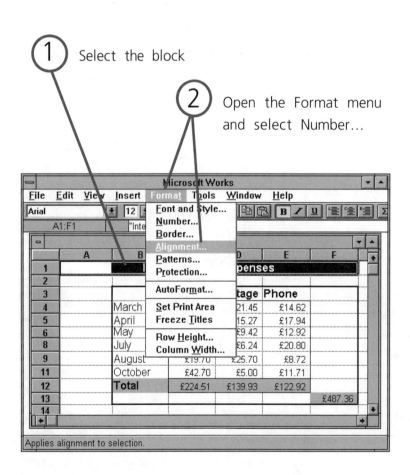

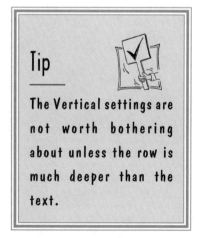

Tip

The Vertical settings are not worth bothering about unless the row is much deeper than the text.

68

General aligns text to the left and numbers to the right.

Left, **Right** and **Centre** are the same as in the Word Processor.

Fill repeats whatever is in the first cell to fill the selected block. Use it to create dividing lines of characters.

Centre across selection takes whatever is in the first cell and positions it centrally in the selected block.

Wordwrap takes a long string of text and breaks it into multiple lines, to fit within the width of the cell. You may well need to increase the height to make all the lines visible.

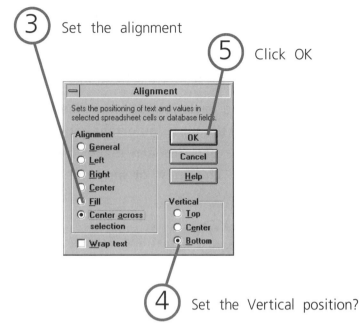

③ Set the alignment

⑤ Click OK

④ Set the Vertical position?

Centred in the block B1:E1

One * set to Fill this block

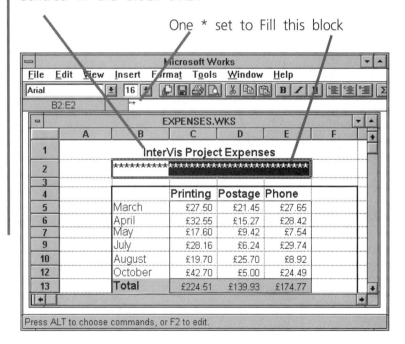

69

Borders and Patterns

Borders can help to create a more visual structure to your sheet. Placed around a block, they will group the contents into one unit; placed along one side or beneath, they will separate values from their headings or totals.

Patterns and coloured backgrounds can make focus the readers' attention on the most important aspects of the sheet – though some patterns can make the contents virtually unreadable. This may, or may not, be a bad thing.

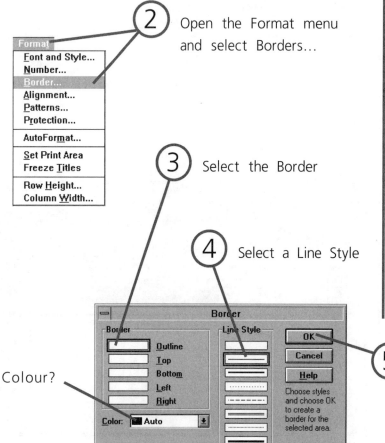

② Open the Format menu and select Borders...

③ Select the Border

④ Select a Line Style

Colour?

⑤ Click OK

Basic steps

❏ **To add borders:**

1 Highlight the cells to be formatted.

2 Open the **Format** menu and select **Borders...**

3 Select the **Borders** which are to have lines.

4 Select the **Line Style**, and **Colour** if wanted.

5 Click **OK**.

❏ **To remove borders:**

1 Highlight the cells to be tidied up.

2 Check the **Border** with the unwanted lines. (If in doubt, check them all.)

3 Select **None** from the **Line Style**.

Basic steps

☐ **To add a pattern**

1 Highlight the cells to be formatted.

2 Open the **Format** menu and select **Patterns**...

3 Click the arrow to open the **Pattern** list, and click on the one you want.

4 Set the **Foreground** and **Background** colours.

5 Check the **Sample**, and if you are happy, click **OK**.

For coloured text, use Color option in the Font and Style dialog box.

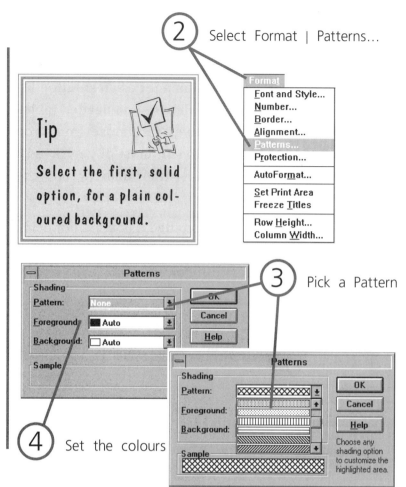

Select Format | Patterns...

Pick a Pattern

Set the colours

Tip

Select the first, solid option, for a plain coloured background.

Choose any shading option to customize the highlighted area.

Patterns can make the contents unreadable

Autoformats

The spreadsheet's Autoformats, like the word processor's Quick Formats, offer an instant design solution for common situations. They are all based on headed tables or lists, but with 14 alternatives to choose from, you should find something there to suit most of your needs. The formatting includes that of the numbers, and the style of text, as well as shading and borders.

Colours and shades are best avoided if you are not using a colour printer, as they are likely to be translated into dot patterns, making text difficult to read.

1 Select the table or list to be formatted, including its headers and totals.

2 Open the **Format** menu and select **Autoformat...**

3 Pick a **Table format** from the list, checking its appearance with the **Sample**.

4 If it is a simple list, click on the **No totals** option

5 Click **OK**.

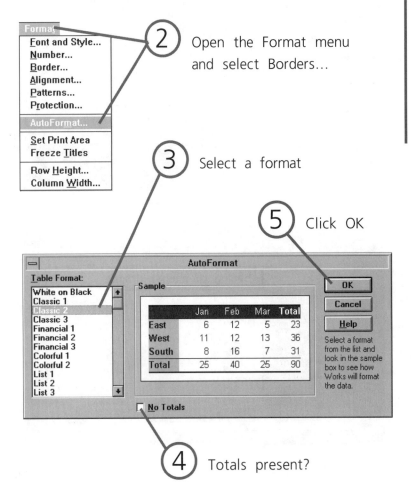

Open the Format menu and select Borders...

Select a format

Click OK

Totals present?

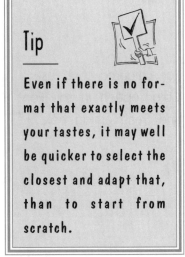

Tip

Even if there is no format that exactly meets your tastes, it may well be quicker to select the closest and adapt that, than to start from scratch.

Writing formulae

Basic steps

☐ **To total a range:**

1 Click on the cell below the column (or to the right of the row).

2 Click on the Σ *Autosum* button.

3 You will see that the column (or row) is highlighted, and that there is =SUM(*range*) in the formula line.

4 If range covers the right cells, click ✓ or press **[Enter]** to accept the formula.

You won't get far with a spreadsheet without writing formulae, but at least Works makes it a fairly painless business. If you just want to total a column or row of figures, it only takes a click of a button. Other calculations take a little more effort, but point and click references, and readily-accessible lists of functions simplify the process and reduce the chance of errors.

A formula starts with the = sign and can contain a mixture of cell or range references, numbers, text and functions, joined by operators. These include the arithmetic symbols /*-+^ and a few others.

Examples of simple formulae:

= 4 * C1   4 times the contents of cell C1

= B3+B4   the value in B3 added to that in B4

=SUM(A5:A12) the sum of the values in cells A5 to A12.

References can be typed into the formula line, or pulled in by clicking on a cell or highlighting a range.

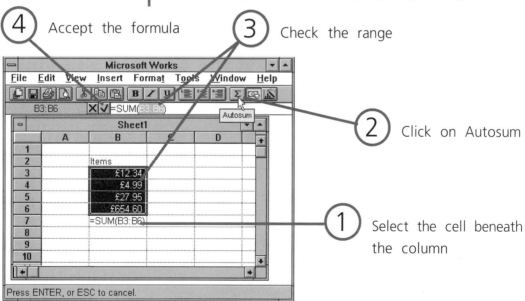

④ Accept the formula

③ Check the range

② Click on Autosum

① Select the cell beneath the column

❑ **To write a formula:**

1 Click on the cell where the formula is to go.

2 Type =

3 Type the number, or point and click to get a cell reference.

4 Type an operator symbol /*-+

5 Type the next number, or select the next reference.

6 Repeat steps 4 and 5, as necessary, to complete the formula.

7 Click ☑ or press [Enter].

Take note

SUM is just one of many built-in functions for manipulating text and numbers. See next page.

② Type **=**

③ Number or reference

④ Type an operator

⑤ Number or reference

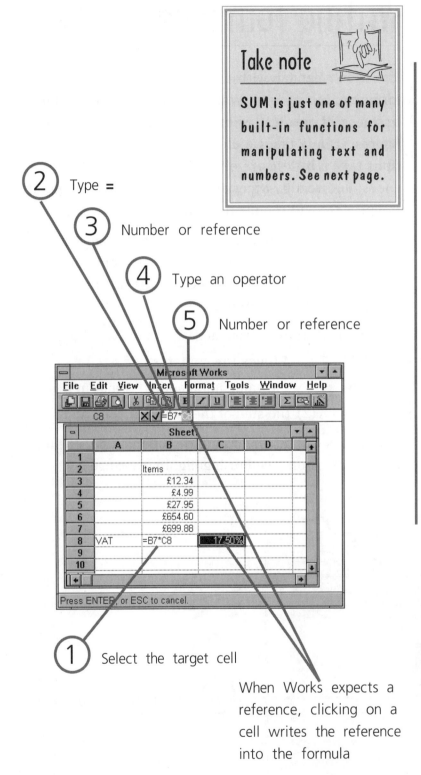

① Select the target cell

When Works expects a reference, clicking on a cell writes the reference into the formula

Tip

If a cell displays the formula, not its result, there is an error in it. Select the cell and press [F2] to edit it.

Basic steps

❑ **To name a range:**

1 Select the cell or the range.

2 Open the **Insert** menu and select **Range Names..**

3 Type a suitable name into the top slot.

4 Click **OK**.

❑ **To remove a name:**

1 Open the **Insert** menu and select **Range Names..**

2 Highlight the name in the list.

3 Click **Delete**.

Take note

Deleting a name does not affect anything else. The contents of the cells will be untouched, and references will replace any names that were used in formulae.

Cell and range references are hard to remember, and if you reorganise the layout of the spreadsheet, you may have to learn them all again. To make life simpler, Works allows you to give meaningful names to cells and ranges. Use them. They will make your formulae more readable, and if you want to transfer data into a word processed document, you can only do this with named ranges.

(1) Highlight the range

(2) Select Insert | Range Names

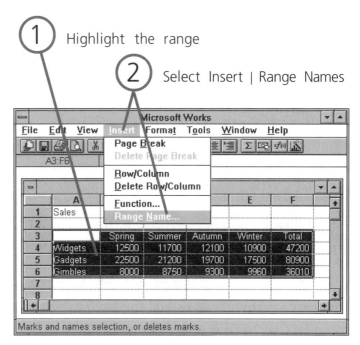

(3) Type a name

(4) Click OK

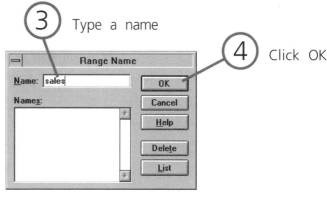

Functions

A function takes one or more number of text values, performs some kind of process on them and gives a new value in return. It may be a simple process, as with SUM, which adds up a range of number. It may be a familiar one such as SIN, which gives the sine of an angle. It may be a complex process that you wouldn't meet anywhere except on a spreadsheet. PMT, for example, will give you the regular repayment on a mortgage. There is no room here to look at these functions properly, but what we can do is cover the basics of how to use them.

All functions come with dummy arguments in their brackets, e.g. SIN(x) or COUNT(RangeRef0,RangeRef1,...). These tell you the type of values that you should be supplying to the function. Replace the dummies with suitable cell or range references, and the function is ready to roll.

The most common dummy arguments are:

x standing for a number or the reference of a cell that contains a number

RangeRef0   to be replaced by a range reference

... indicates that you can repeat the last type of value. For example, COUNT(RangeRef0,RangeRef1,...) tells you how many cells in one or more ranges contain something. It could be written:

COUNT(A2:A12)   for one partial column

COUNT(A1:E12)   for one block

COUNT(A2:A12,   E5:H10) counting two ranges.

Basic steps

1 Select the cell into which the formula should go.

2 Open the **Insert** menu and select **Function...** or click the Insert Function ⬚ button, if you have added it to your toolbar.

3 Pick the **Category** of function from the panel on the left.

4 Scroll through the list to find the one you want, and click on it.

5 Click **OK** to copy it to the formula line.

6 Replace the dummy argument(s) with suitable values or references.

7 Enter the formula.

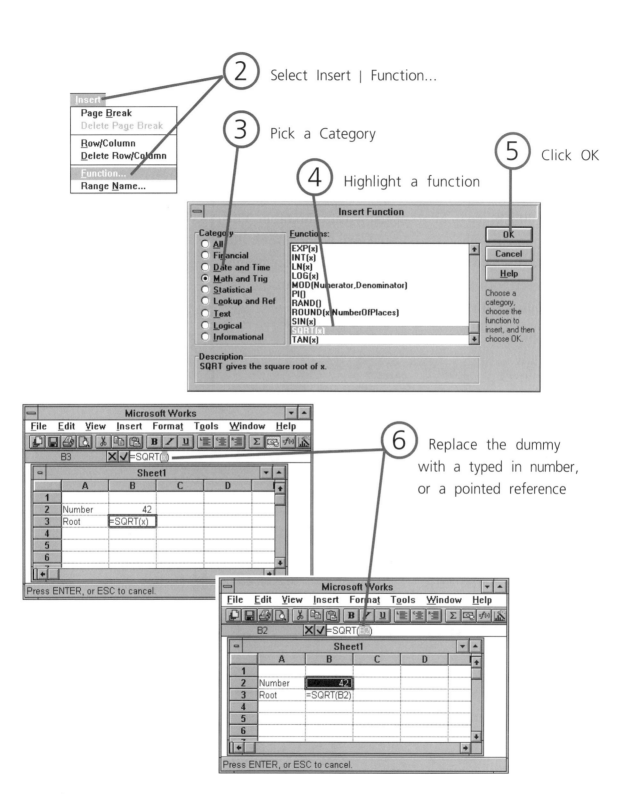

② Select Insert | Function...

③ Pick a Category

⑤ Click OK

④ Highlight a function

Insert
Page **B**reak
Delete Page Break
Row/Column
Delete Row/Column
Function...
Range **N**ame...

Insert Function

Category
- ○ **A**ll
- ○ Fi**n**ancial
- ○ **D**ate and Time
- ● **M**ath and Trig
- ○ **S**tatistical
- ○ **L**ookup and Ref
- ○ **T**ext
- ○ Lo**g**ical
- ○ **I**nformational

Functions:
EXP(x)
INT(x)
LN(x)
LOG(x)
MOD(Numerator,Denominator)
PI()
RAND()
ROUND(x,NumberOfPlaces)
SIN(x)
SQRT(x)
TAN(x)

OK
Cancel
Help

Choose a category, choose the function to insert, and then choose OK.

Description
SQRT gives the square root of x.

Microsoft Works

File Edit View Insert Format Tools Window Help

B3   X ✓ =SQRT(x)

Sheet1

	A	B	C	D
1				
2	Number	42		
3	Root	=SQRT(x)		
4				
5				
6				

Press ENTER, or ESC to cancel.

⑥ Replace the dummy with a typed in number, or a pointed reference

Microsoft Works

File Edit View Insert Format Tools Window Help

B2   X ✓ =SQRT(B2)

Sheet1

	A	B	C	D
1				
2	Number	42		
3	Root	=SQRT(B2)		
4				
5				
6				

Press ENTER, or ESC to cancel.

Lookup functions

One category of functions that are worth exploration are the Lookup functions. They can be really useful, and in getting to grips with these you will master most of the techniques you need for working with other functions.

A Lookup function will scan through a list of items in a table, to find a key item, then pick a value out of the corresponding place in another list within the table. The example opposite shows a simple price and stock list being used by two Lookup formulae. When an item's name is typed into a key cell, the functions scan the list and pick out its price and stock level.

Basic steps

❏ **To use VLOOKUP:**

1 Create a table of data, with index values on the left.

2 Pick a cell into which you will write the key value and type in something which is in the table. This will be used to test the formulae.

3 Select the cell which will hold the formula.

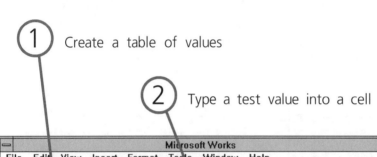

① Create a table of values

② Type a test value into a cell

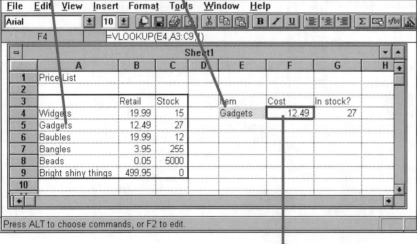

③ Select the formula's cell

4   Call up the **Insert Function...** dialog box.

5   Click on the **Lookup and Ref** category, select **VLOOKUP**.

6   Click **OK** to copy it into the formula line.

7   The *LookupValue* will be highlighted. Select the cell containing your key value to replace this dummy with the reference.

8   Highlight *RangeRef*, then select the range that covers the table.

9   Delete *ColNum* and type 1 to get the value from the first column to the right of the index values, or 2 to get the value in the second column.

10 Click ☑ to accept the formula.

There are two similar functions.

● **HLOOKUP** works with tables where the index values are written across the top of the table;

● **VLOOKUP** expects the index values to be down the left side fo the table.

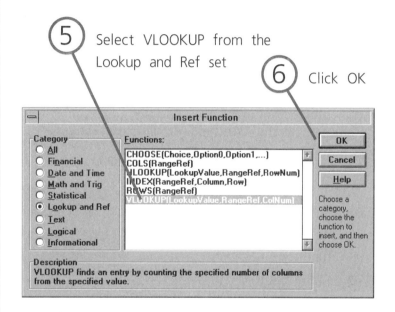

(5) Select VLOOKUP from the Lookup and Ref set

(6) Click OK

=VLOOKUP(D3,RangeRef,ColNum)

After the first dummy, you will have to highlight the dummies yourself before you can replace them with a pulled-in reference.

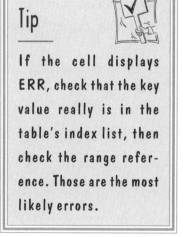

Tip

If the cell displays ERR, check that the key value really is in the table's index list, then check the range reference. Those are the most likely errors.

Summary

❑ A spreadsheet is a grid of **cells**, each identified by its **row** and **column reference**. A cell's contents and its screen display may differ. Formulae are shown by their resulting values; text may be cropped short and numbers shown as hashes in a narrow column.

❑ Rows and columns can be **selected** by their header numbers and letters; blocks are selected by dragging highlight.

❑ The appearance of the sheet can be enhanced by the use of **fonts, alignments, borders** and **patterns**.

❑ **Numbers** can be displayed in different formats.

❑ The **Autoformat** options provide a quick way to give a professional finish to tables.

❑ **Formulae** all start with = and may include a mixture of text and number values, cell and range reference and functions.

❑ There is a wide range of **functions**, organised into several categories. They are easily accessed through the **Insert Function** dialog box.

❑ The **Lookup** functions allow you to write formulae that will extract information from a table.

6 Working with tables

Copying and filling

The usual **Edit Copy**, **Cut** and **Paste** facilities are available here, as anywhere else in Windows, but there are also alternatives which may be better. Much of the time, the copying that you want to do, is of formulae to create a table. For this, the **Fill Right** and **Fill Down** commands are quicker and simpler. They will take the formula in the first cell of a range and copy it into all the other cells, adjusting the references as they go, so that the formulae continue to apply to the same relative cells.

For example, if you had a formula in C2 that read:

$= A2 * B2$

When this is copied down into C3, the formula will read:

$= A3 * B3$

As you would normally want the same type of formula all down the table, this automatic adjustment of references is generally a good thing.

❏ **To Fill Down:**

1 Write a formula in the cell at the top of the table.

2 Select the range, starting with your formula cell and continuing to the bottom of the table.

3 Open the **Edit** menu and select **Fill Down...** or click if you have added it to the toolbar.

4 Check any of the new formulae and you should see that their references have been adjusted to suit their new positions.

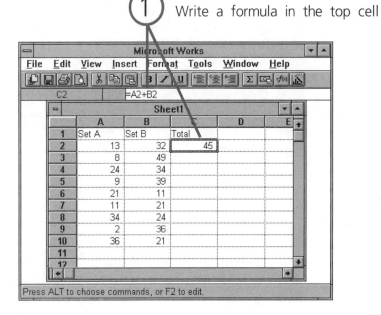

① Write a formula in the top cell

Tip

Fill Right will copy a formula across the base of a table. Add its button to the toolbar for quicker copying.

Fixed references

You may want to copy a formula, but keep a references unchanged. For example, you might want to calculate the VAT on each item in a table, and the VAT rate is stored in one cell.

To keep a reference unchanged, edit the formula and type a $ sign before the column letter and row number.

If C1 held this:

= A1 * B1

when copied into C2 it would read:

= A2 * B1

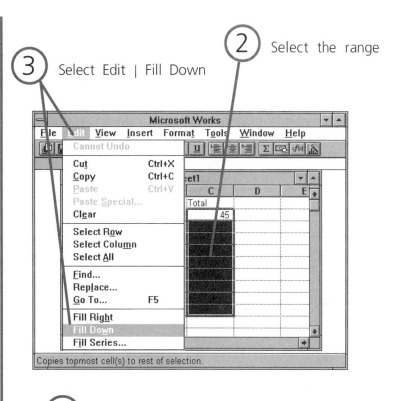

③ Select Edit | Fill Down

② Select the range

④ Check the references in any formula

Fill Series

The third option of this type, **Fill Series**, does not copy, but it does create a sequence of numbers or dates. When you are setting up a schedule of work, or any kind of numbered list, it can save a great deal of tedious typing. All the command needs is a starting numebr or date, and a place to put the series.

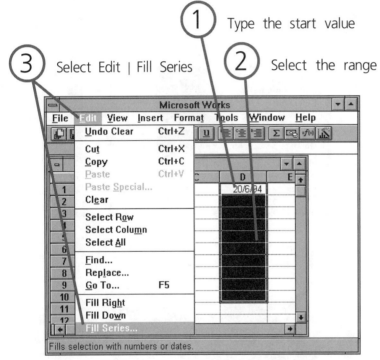

Type the start value

Select Edit | Fill Series

Select the range

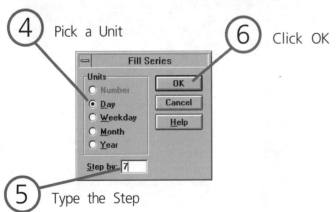

Pick a Unit

Click OK

Type the Step

1 Type into the top or leftmost cell the first number or date.

2 Select the range which the series will occupy.

3 Open the **Edit** menu and select **Fill Series...** or click on if you have added it to your toolbar.

4 At the dialog box, you will be offered a selection of intervals if you are working with dates. Click the **Unit** that you want.

5 Type in the **Step by** value.

6 Click **OK**.

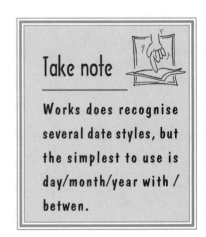

Take note

Works does recognise several date styles, but the simplest to use is day/month/year with / betwen.

Cut and Paste Copying

1 Highlight the cell(s) to be copied.

2 Open the **Edit** menu and select **Copy**, or click on

3 Highlight the range into which the cells are to be duplicated.

4 Open the **Edit** menu and select **Paste**, or click on

If you want to copy formulae or data anywhere other than down or right, you must turn to the **Edit | Copy** and **Paste** commands.

For straightforward one-to-one copying, their use is exactly the same as elsewhere in Windows, but you are not limited to this. You can also do one-to-many copying – duplicating a formula throughout a range.

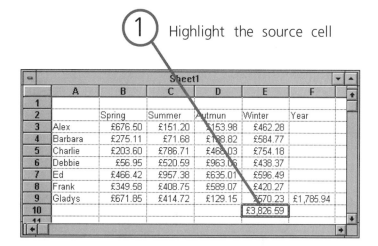

(1) Highlight the source cell

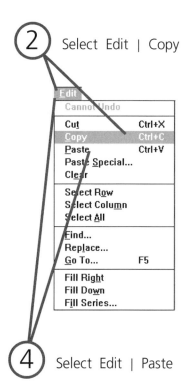

(2) Select Edit | Copy

(4) Select Edit | Paste

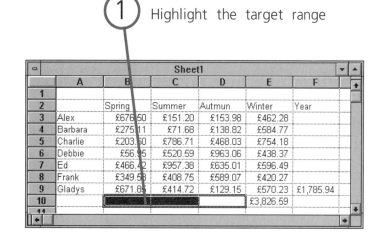

(1) Highlight the target range

Heights and widths

The spreadsheet grid is not fixed. You can adjust the layout and the column widths and row heights. You can make them bigger to give more room for the contents of cells or to create more space between items, or smaller, to fit more on a page. You can even **hide** rows or columns by adjusting their heights and widths down to zero.

Height and width adjustments are essentially cosmetic. They may improve the presentation of the spreadsheet and make it easier to read, but they will not affect any of the underlying structure on calculations in any way.

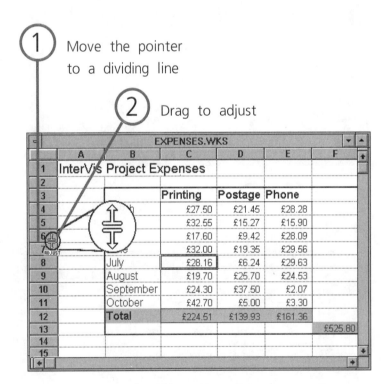

(1) Move the pointer to a dividing line

(2) Drag to adjust

- [ ] **To adjust a single row:**

1 Move the pointer to the dividing line **below** the row you want to adjust.

2 When the pointer changes to the ADJUST double arrow, hold down the mouse button and drag to the desired height.

- [ ] **To adjust a single column:**

1 Move the pointer to the dividing line **to the right** of the column you want to adjust.

2 Drag the ADJUST pointer to the desired width.

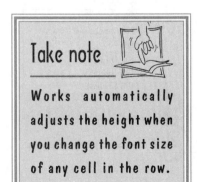

Take note

Works automatically adjusts the height when you change the font size of any cell in the row.

Basic steps

☐ To adjust a set of columns:

1 Select the columns by their letters, or select any block of cells that spans the set.

2 Open the **Format** menu and select **Column Width...**

3 Type in a new value in the dialog box. The range is from 0, which will hide them all, and 79, at which one column will fill the screen.

4 Click **OK**.

☐ To adjust a set of rows:

1 Follow the steps above, but using the **Format | Row Height...** command. Heights are given in point sizes. The default is 12 to fit 10 point text.

Multiple adjustments

Dragging the adjust pointer will only change the size of one row or column at a time. If you want to adjust the size of a set of them in one fell swoop, you must tackle it through the Format menu.

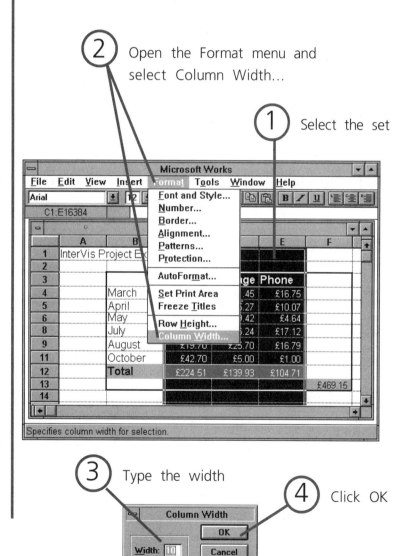

② Open the Format menu and select Column Width...

① Select the set

③ Type the width

④ Click OK

Hidden rows & columns

You may have a spreadsheet which contains confidential material, but which you want to be able to use it for public consumption. An invoicing sheet, for example, might have formulae and percentages to calculate your overheads. You want to print customers' copies from this sheet, but without revealing your secrets. The problem can be solved by hiding the rows or columns that contain the sensitive data. Of course, if you drag a height or width to zero by accident, the hiding becomes the problem!

To recover hidden rows and columns, you must first select them. You cannot do this with the mouse as you cannot see them. The only way is to use the **Go To** facility to leap to a cell in the hidden area. The height or width can then be restored via the **Format** menu.

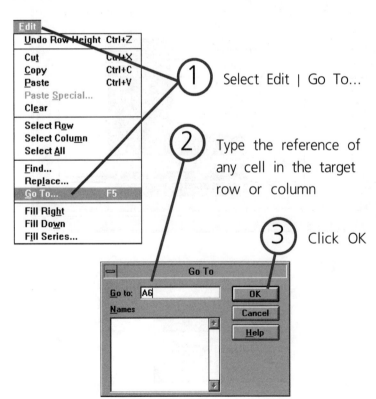

Select Edit | Go To...

Type the reference of any cell in the target row or column

Click OK

□ **To hide rows or columns:**

1 Drag the dividing line up or left until it meets the line on the opposite side of the row or column.

□ **To restore hidden rows or columns:**

1 Open the **Edit** menu and select **Go To**.

2 Type in the reference of any cell in the row.

3 Click **OK**.

4 By going to the cell, you have selected it, and its row or column. You can now use the Format menu to adjust the height or width, (see the previous page.)

Adjusting the layout

□ **To move a row:**

1 Click on the number to select the row.

2 Move the pointer into the grid area, near the bottom of the row.

3 When the pointer changes from the cross to the DRAG arrow, hold down the mouse button and move the row to its new place.

4 Release the button and the row will insert itself between the existing rows.

□ **To move a column:**

Follow the same steps as above, but look for the DRAG arrow by the right of the column.

① Select the whole row

② Get the drag arrow

③ Pull to its new place

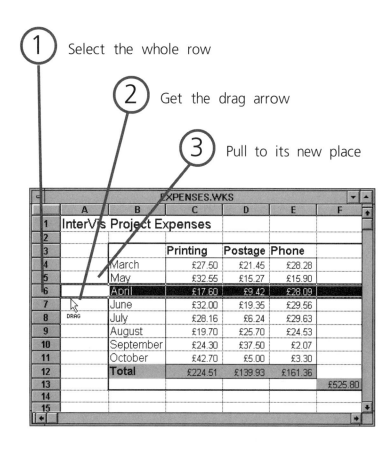

Take note

When you move any cells containing formulae, the cell reference will be adjusted so that the formulae continue to have the same effect.

Moving blocks

Moving blocks of cells is different from moving rows or columns. The process is the same, and cell references in formulae are adjusted in the same way, but the effects on the sheet are different.

When you move – or *drag and drop* in the jargon – a full row or column into a new position, existing lines make space for it, and the hole that it left is closed up. When you move a block, you lift its data and formulae out of the cells and place them in the new location. A hole is left behind, and the moved contents will overwrite anything that was there before.

Basic steps

❑ **To move a block:**

1 Select the block.

2 Place the cross pointer over any of the edges or corners to get the DRAG arrow.

3 Drag the outline to its new position, taking care not to overlap any wanted data.

4 Release to drop the block into its new position.

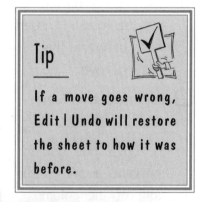

Tip

If a move goes wrong, Edit I Undo will restore the sheet to how it was before.

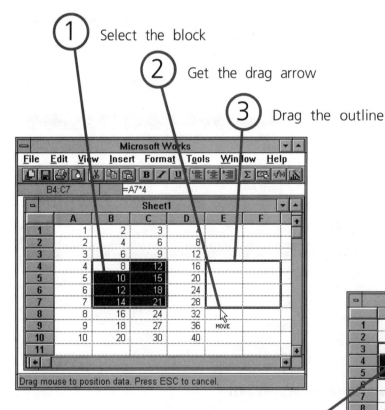

① Select the block

② Get the drag arrow

③ Drag the outline

The moved block will overwrite existing data

Basic steps

Inserting and deleting

❏ **To insert rows or columns:**

1 Select as many rows/ columns as you want to insert, at the place where you want them to go.

2 Open the **Insert** menu and select **Row/Column.** Existing rows will move down, columns move right to make room.

❏ **To delete rows or columns:**

1 Select the rows/columns you want to delete.

2 Open the **Insert** menu and select **Delete Row/Column.**

You can only insert or delete rows or columns, and not blocks within the sheet. Bear in mind that it is the *whole* row, or column, that is removed. If the occupied area of your sheet extends beyond the visible screen, check along the line to see if there is any data elsewhere that you would prefer not to lose.

There are optional buttons to cover all four insert/delete row/column combinations. If you are faced with an extensive restructuring of your sheet, it may be worth adding these to the toolbar.

Insert row

Insert column

Delete row

Delete column

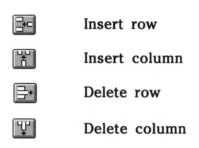

Both Insert and Delete commands are on the Insert menu

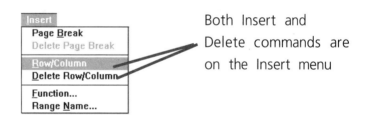

If a single cell or a block is selected when you give an Insert or Delete command, you will be asked to specify row or column.

Sorting

Where you have a table of data organised, database-wise, so that each row holds details of one contact, customer, stock item or whatever, this can be sorted into order. The sort can be ascending or descending, numeric or alphabetic, and can be based on up to three columns. A contact list, for example, could be sorted first by County, then by Town and finally by Name.

❑ **To sort on a single column:**

1 Select the block to be sorted

2 Open the **Tools** menu and select **Sort Rows...**

3 At the dialog box, type in the letter of the column on which to sort.

4 If **Descending** order is wanted, set this option.

5 Click **OK**.

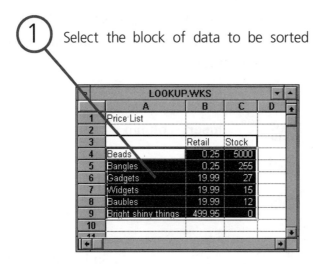

Select the block of data to be sorted

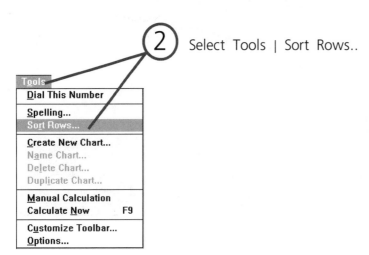

Select Tools | Sort Rows..

Tip

When selecting the block, take care not to include any headings that you have added to your columns.

❏ **To sort on several columns:**

1 Follow steps 1 & 2 as for single column sorts.

2 Repeat steps 3 & 4 for each column, working left to right in order of importance.

③ Type the key column

④ Ascend or Descend?

⑤ Click OK

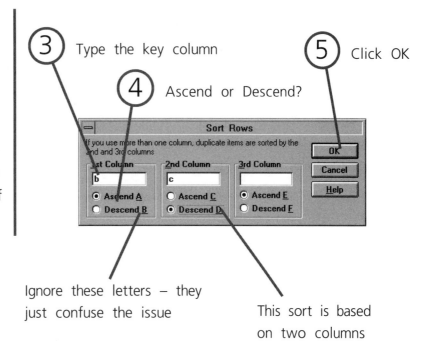

Ignore these letters – they just confuse the issue

This sort is based on two columns

The rows have been first sorted into *Ascending* order of Price, then on *Descending* order of number in Stock.

Summary

❑ Data and formulae can be copied either with **Copy** and **Paste** or with the **Fill Right** and **Fill Down** commands.

❑ When formulae are copied, cell and range references are normally adjusted to suit the new positions. If required, references can be absolute, so that they are not changes when the formula is copied.

❑ **Edit | Paste** can be used to duplicate a cell or range of single cells.

❑ You can adjust the **height** of rows and the **width** of columns. If they are reduced to zero, the lines become hidden.

❑ **Hidden** rows and columns can be restored by using **Go To,** to move to a cell in the hidden area, and then increasing the height or width.

❑ Rows, columns and blocks can be **moved** to another position in the sheet. Existing rows and columns will shuffle up to make room for the moved ones. When blocks are moved, they will overwrite any existing data.

❑ Rows and columns can be **inserted** or **deleted**.

❑ Blocks of data can be **sorted** on the values held in key columns.

7 Working with charts

Charts from tables

Graphs and charts can bring out the underlying patterns in sets of numbers, and with Works you have a good range of charting styles, to cope with all kinds of data. Creating a chart could scarcely be simpler, and once created, a chart can easily be adapted. A few minutes' experimenting with different styles should be enough to find one that best displays the underlying patterns.

To create a chart, you must first have a table of figures. If this has headings above and to the left, Works will use them as labels on the chart.

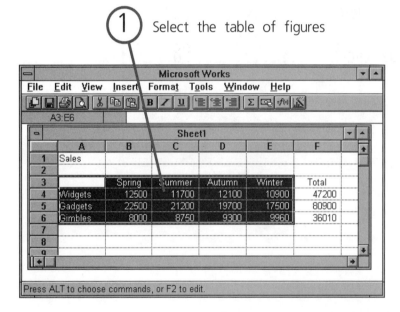

① Select the table of figures

1 Select the block of cells containing the figures and their headings.

2 Open the **Tools** menu and select **Create New Chart...** or click on the toolbar.

3 Check the **Sample** and if this is what you want, click **OK** to close the dialog box.

4 To change the Type of chart, pull down the list and select one from there. (N.B. It can be changed later.)

5 If your series run down the columns, click on the **Down** option.

Take note

A *series* is a set of numbers that will make a line or a set of bars. You can have up to 6 series in one chart.

6 If the First column does not contain headings, click on **Category**.

7 If the **First row** does not contain headings, click on **Y values**.

8 Click **OK**.

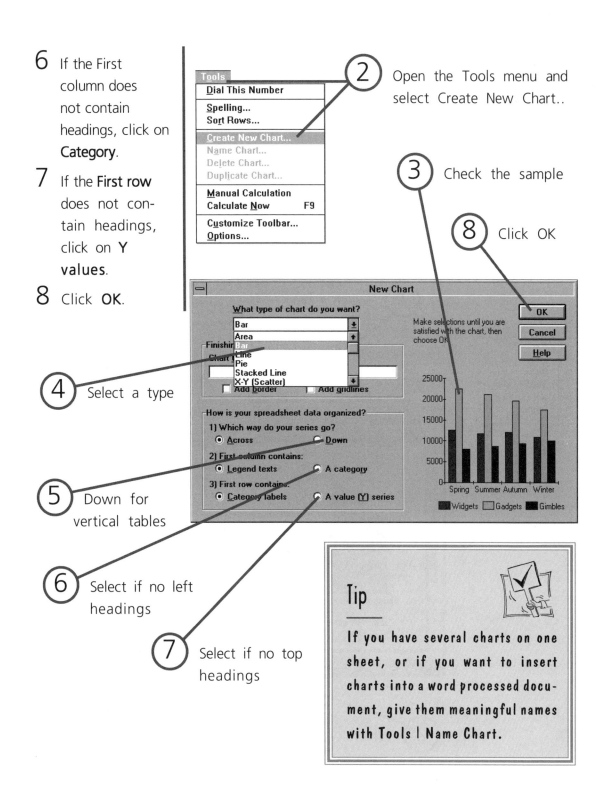

Tools
Dial This Number
Spelling...
Sort Rows...
Create New Chart...
Name Chart...
Delete Chart...
Duplicate Chart...
Manual Calculation
Calculate Now   F9
Customize Toolbar...
Options...

② Open the Tools menu and select Create New Chart..

③ Check the sample

⑧ Click OK

New Chart

What type of chart do you want?
Bar
Area
Finishir Bar
Chart   Line
         Pie
         Stacked Line
         X-Y (Scatter)
         Add border   Add gridlines

④ Select a type

How is your spreadsheet data organized?
1) Which way do your series go?
   ⊙ Across   ○ Down
2) First column contains:
   ⊙ Legend texts   ○ A category
3) First row contains:
   ⊙ Category labels ○ A value (Y) series

⑤ Down for vertical tables

⑥ Select if no left headings

⑦ Select if no top headings

Make selections until you are satisfied with the chart, then choose OK

OK
Cancel
Help

25000
20000
15000
10000
5000
0
   Spring Summer Autumn Winter
■Widgets □Gadgets ■Gimbles

Tip

If you have several charts on one sheet, or if you want to insert charts into a word processed document, give them meaningful names with Tools I Name Chart.

Tailor-made charts

A chart appears in a window of its own, not within the spreadsheet, and when that window is on top, you will see a new set of buttons in the toolbar. Most of these are for selecting different chart types, and there is another new one that will take you back to the spreadsheet at the site of the first series.

If you want to alter any item on the chart, it must be done through one of the menu commands. You cannot select items for formatting in the usual way.

Basic steps

❑ **To change the type:**

1 Open the **Gallery** menu and select a type from there or click on its button.

2 A palette of variations will open. Highlight the one you want.

3 Click OK.

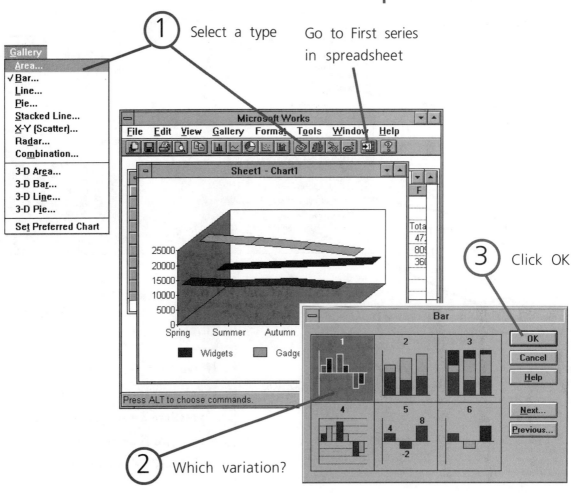

To change patterns:

1 Open the **Format** menu and select **Patterns and Colors...**

2 At the dialog box, click on the **Series** you want to change.

3 Select a fill or line **Color** and a **Pattern**.

4 Click **Format** to fix your choices.

5 Repeat steps 2 to 4 for all the series.

6 **Close** the dialog box.

Tip

If you have a black and white printer, check the effect of your colours and patterns by selecting *Display as Printed* from the *View* menu, or take a **Print Preview**. What looks good in colour may be awful in black and white.

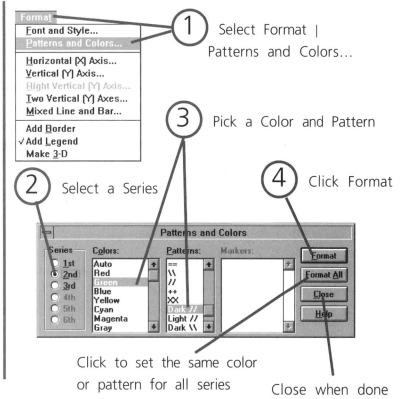

(1) Select Format | Patterns and Colors...

(3) Pick a Color and Pattern

(2) Select a Series

(4) Click Format

Click to set the same color or pattern for all series

Close when done

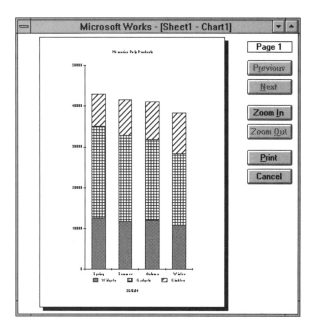

Summary

- Works can take a table of figures and produce a chart from it for you.

- There are a wide variety of chart **types**, designed to meet a range of display needs. They can be selected from the toolbar buttons.

- Charts can be given meaningful **Names** to make them easier to find later.

- To change the appearance of any items on a chart, you must work through the **Format** menu commands.

- **Colours** and fill **patterns** that work well on screen, do not always work as well when printed. Check your choices with **Print Preview** or by switching to **Display as Printed** view.

8 Working with data

Creating a database

A database is a collection of *records*, each of which will contain data about one person, company, stock item or whatever. The record is split into *fields*, each of which will hold the same kind of data in every record.

The database can be viewed as a *List*, where it will look like a table in a spreadsheet, with each record occupying its own row, and the fields running down the columns. It can also be viewed as a set of *Forms*, where the data for each record is laid out as it might be in a card-index system.

By running *queries*, you can pull out groups of records that have specified values in particular fields. You could find, for example, all your customers who lived in Macclesfield or those stock items need to be reordered.

The reports that can be produced from a database may include all items, or a set that have been selected by a query. They may show all the available data for each record, or only that from selected fields. In this way, the same database can produce mailing labels to send a circular to all your customers, and a list of those who owe money, showing the amounts and the age of each debt.

Data can be copied to and from a spreadsheet, so that you can perform there the calculations that cannot be done in the database. Names, addresses and other data from a database can be combined with standard letters to produced mailshots. (See *Mail Merge*, page 133.)

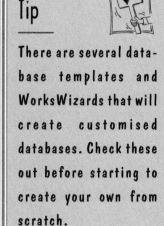

Tip

There are several database templates and WorksWizards that will create customised databases. Check these out before starting to create your own from scratch.

Preparing the data

The most important stage in creating a database takes place off-screen. You must have your data organised thoroughly first, before you start to think about form and report designs.

The key questions are:

- What do you want to store?
- What do you want to be able to get out of it?

There are two main aspects to this:

Data must be broken down into the smallest units that you might want to sort on or search for. If you are storing people's names, for instance, you would normally break them into three fields, Title, Initials (or Forenames) and Surname. The records could then be sorted alphabetically (by Surname), and you could search for someone by their Forename or Surname. It is crucial to get this right from the very start, as you cannot split data up , once it has been typed in.

The space you allocate to any field should be long enough to take the largest item that might go there. How long is the longest surname that you want to store? If you don't know in advance, then take a sample of some typical names and add a few more characters to be sure. That is the size of your surname field. This is not as crucial since field sizes can be expanded later without affecting any existing data.

Designing the form

When you start to create a new database, you will be presented with a blank form. The system is waiting for you to add the fields that will create the structure of the database. You can also add headings, notes and other text labels, as well as graphics. Design the form with screen use in mind. You can print it, but most of your printing from the database will be as reports, or mailing labels and mailmerge letters via the word processor.

Fields are added by typing their names where you want the fields to appear. The only difference between field names and other text labels is that the names are followed by a colon. Miss this out and you have a label!

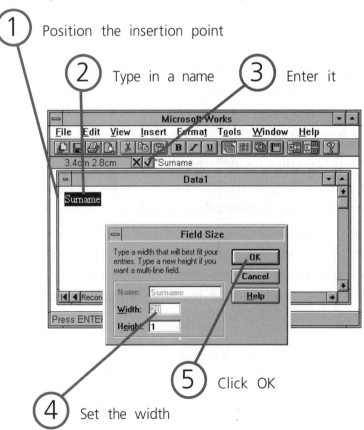

① Position the insertion point

② Type in a name   ③ Enter it

④ Set the width

⑤ Click OK

Basic steps

1 Place the insertion point where you want the field to appear.

2 Type a name for the field, ending with :

3 Press [Enter] or click ☑ to enter the name.

4 At the **Field Size** dialog box, adjust the **Width** to suit the data that will be displayed there. Set the **Height** to 2 or more to spread a long field over several lines.

5 Click **OK**. A dotted line appears beside the name, ready for the field's data.

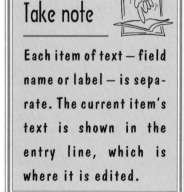

Take note

Each item of text — field name or label — is separate. The current item's text is shown in the entry line, which is where it is edited.

104

Basic steps

Selecting fields and other items

To select a single item:

1 Click on it. This works for field names, data areas, labels and any other objects.

To select a group of adjacent objects:

1 Point to the top left of the enclosing area.

2 Drag to draw an outline around them.

To select a group of scattered items:

1 Click on the first item.

2 Hold [Ctrl] and click on the rest. If you pick one by mistake, click again to deselect it.

As elsewhere in Works, you must select items before you can do anything with them. Once they are selected, you can change their format, move and resize them.

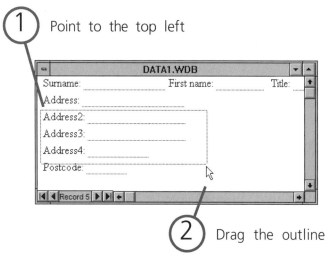

① Point to the top left

② Drag the outline

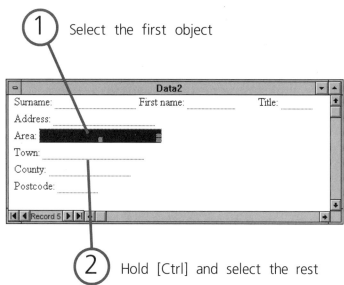

① Select the first object

② Hold [Ctrl] and select the rest

Tip

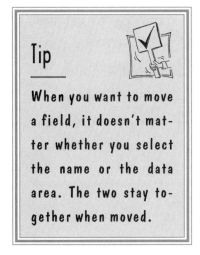

When you want to move a field, it doesn't matter whether you select the name or the data area. The two stay together when moved.

Adjusting the layout

Fields and labels can be moved at any point during the initial design time, or later, after you have started to enter data. The width of fields can also be adjusted if you find that data items are larger – or smaller – than anticipated. Changing the width only changes how much is displayed. It has no effect on the data contained in the fields.

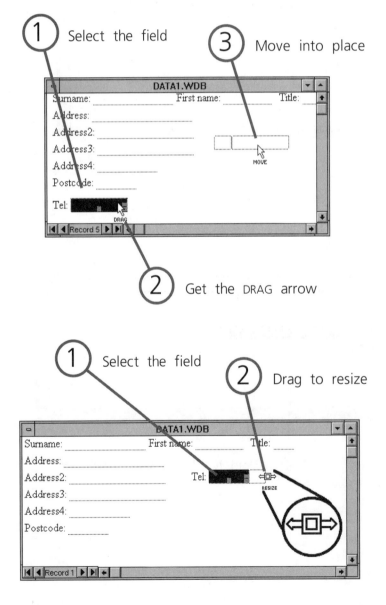

❑ **To move fields:**

1 Select the field, or fields, to be moved.

2 Move the pointer over the field until the DRAG prompt shows.

3 Hold down the mouse button and move to the new location.

4 Release to drop the fields. If they overlap any other fields, it will mess up the display but have no other effect.

❑ **To resize a field:**

1 Select a field - one at a time only.

2 Move the pointer to an edge to get the RESIZE arrow.

3 Drag the outline to required size.

4 Release the button.

106

Basic steps

1 Select the field by clicking on the name or the data area beside it, or select a set of fields together by dragging an outline around them.

2 Open the **Format** menu and click **Show Field Name** to remove the tick.

Hiding field names

The names that you give to fields are not necessarily what you want to use on screen to identify them for your readers. Names like *Address Line 1*, *Address Line 2* are good names, but unnecessary to the user, and while *Pest* (to identify awkward customers) may be meaningful to you, it is not something you would want them to see.

If you do not want the field names to appear on screen, switch them off. If necessary, you can head up the data area with a more presentable label.

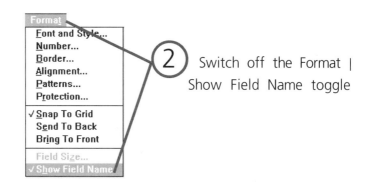

② Switch off the Format | Show Field Name toggle

Take note

If you want to delete a field, you must select it by its name, not its data area. Pressing [Delete] will then remove it from the form and the database. You will be asked to confirm, to prevent accidental deletion.

Presentation

The form can be enhanced in a number of ways:

- **Fonts** and **Alignments** are set here the same as elsewhere – select the items and adjust the settings.

- **Patterns** can be set for fields and the form itself.

- **Borders** can be applied to individual items only, not around a selected set.

- **Rectangles** can be added to make a decorative border around a set of fields.

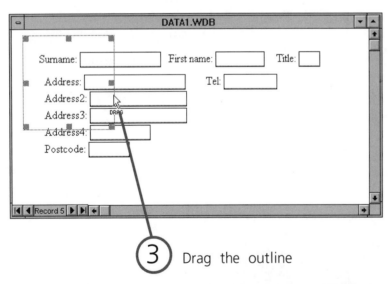

① Get the right part of the form into view

③ Drag the outline

❑ **To add a rectangle:**

1 Adjust the position of the form in the window so that you can see the place where the rectangle is to go.

2 Open the **Insert** menu and select **Rectangle**.

3 A shadow rectangle will be dropped into the top left corner. Drag it and resize it as required.

4 Use the **Borders** and **Patterns** options on the **Format** menu to set the line style for its outline and its background colour.

5 Open the **Format** menu and select **Send to Back** to put the rectangle beneath your fields.

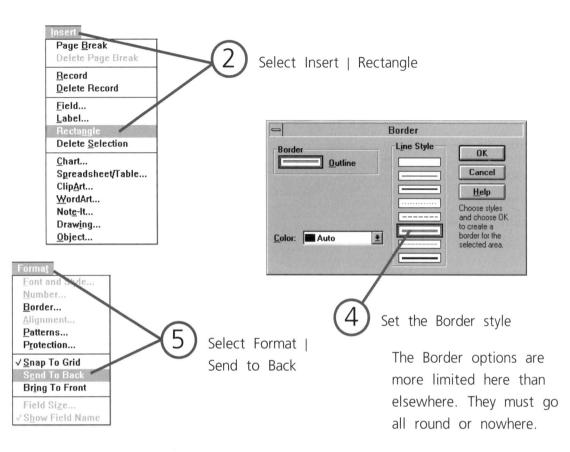

② Select Insert | Rectangle

④ Set the Border style

The Border options are more limited here than elsewhere. They must go all round or nowhere.

⑤ Select Format | Send to Back

Tip

Use the [Ctrl] method for selecting sets of items with a rectangle. If you try to drag an outline you will only succeed in selecting the rectangle itself.

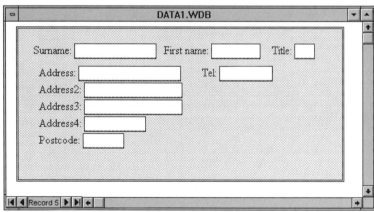

This rectangle was coloured with a light grey dot pattern; the data areas have borders and are filled with white.

Form and List views

The Form view is generally the best one to use when entering data or updating records, for several reasons. You would normally be working on one record at a time, and all its details will be to hand. You can easily move between fields and between adjacent records, either with the mouse or the keyboard.

When you want to get a wider view of the database, or make comparisons between records, switch to List view by clicking 🖩 on the toolbar.

Press [F2] or click here to edit

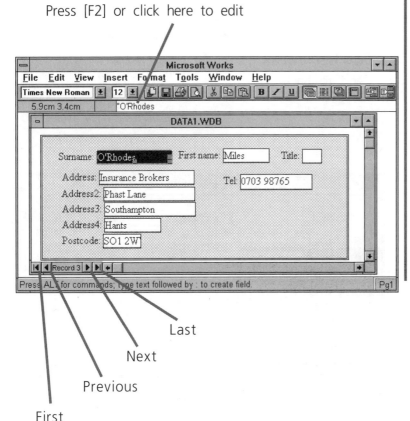

First
Previous
Next
Last

❑ **To edit a field:**

1 Move to the record.

2 Either press **[F2]** or click the insertion point into the text in the entry line.

3 When you have done, click ✔ or press **[Enter]** to accept the changes, click ✖ or press **[Escape]** to leave it unchanged.

❑ **To move with keys:**

[Tab] - next field

[Shift]+[Tab] - previous field

[Ctrl]+[PageDown] - next record

[Ctrl]+[PageUp] - previous record

[Ctrl]+[Home] - first record

[Ctrl]+[End] - last record

Watch out for:

☐ **Fonts, borders and patterns** cannot be applied to a single cell or block. They always apply to whole fields.

☐ **When sorting**, do not select a block. The sort always works on the whole database.

☐ **You cannot move an empty field.** (Don't ask me why not!) If you want to rearrange fields before you start to enter data, stick something into any cell of the field, and then it will move.

☐ **Insert Record** 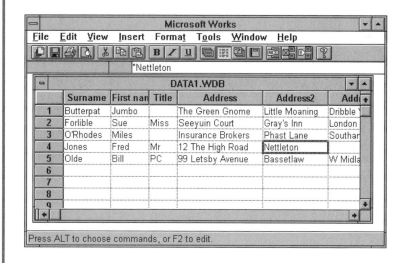 **Delete Record** and **Insert Field** have buttons. There is no button for **Delete Field** as they don't want to make this too easy. Use **Insert | Delete Record**, or delete it in Form view.

Using List view

In List view you can see a screenful of records at a time, though not all of the fields will necessarily be in sight. It is useful when you want to check, or edit, the values in the same fields of different records, and it is simpler to hunt through the database when you can see 15 or 20 records at a time.

The view looks like a spreadsheet, and is handled in much the same way. Things are not exactly the same – the main differences are given on the left.

You can adjust the heights of records and the widths of fields, and note that the changes you make here are not carried over into the form view. You can also move, insert and delete records and fields. All of these operations are carried out as with the rows and columns of the spreadsheet. (See *Adjusting the layout*, page 89.)

Searching for records

If you want to find a record, or pick out a set of records that share some common values, then you must create a Query. In this you define what value, or range of values, you are looking for in a particular field. At the simplest you might look for the person with the surname "Jones", or pick out all those customers that owed you money. If you want to get more complicated, you might set up a query to find, for example, those clients in Manchester that did not owe you money and hadn't received a vist from the rep in the last month.

The queries are saved with the database and can be recalled and reused later, so even if it takes you a little while to phrase the query to pick out exactly the right set of records, at least you will only have to do it once.

	DEBTORS.WDB		
	Customer	**Amount Owing**	**Credit Limit**
1	Dodger & Bodger	£748.56	£500.00
2	Jack McArup	£0.00	£1,000.00
3	M.T. Poquet Ltd	£979.74	£1,000.00
4	Acme Inc	£2,547.90	£2,000.00
5	Bill Derwal	-£27.50	£250.00

The example queries shown here are based on this set of records.

Take note

Comparisons can be with set values, such as "Credit Limit is less than 500", or "Customer is equal to Jack McArup", or with the values in other fields, for example "Amount Owing is greater than Credit Limit"

1 Open the **Tools** menu and select **Create New Query...** or click [?] to open the **New Query** dialog box.

2 Give the query a name to remind you about what sort of records it finds.

3 Pull down the **Choose a field** list, and pick the field that contains the values that you are looking for.

4 Pull down the **How to compare** list and pick a comparison. If it is an exact match, stick with *is equal to.*

5 Type into the **Value to compare** slot what you are looking for.

6 Click **Apply Now**

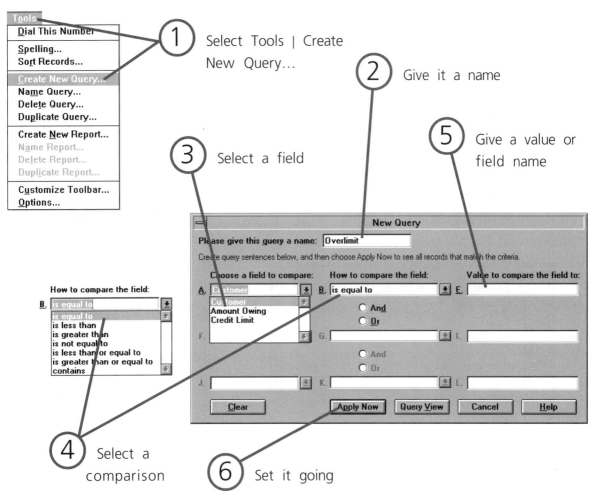

Select Tools | Create
New Query...

Give it a name

Give a value or
field name

Select a field

Select a
comparison

Set it going

Query view (see right) is the same
as Form view, but with the query
statements written into the relevant
fields. If you are happy writing
logical expressions using symbols, it
may be the quickest way to set up
queries. The New Query dialog box
is a friendlier way to do the job.

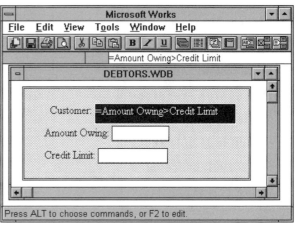

Working with queries

When you apply a query for the very first time, you may be taken aback by the result – especially if you have been working in List view. Instead of having a screen full of records, you may well be faced with only the odd one or two! Where have all the other 10,000 of your records gone? Don't panic. They are all safe, it's just that only ones on display are those that match the requirements of the query. You can bring all the records back into view, or switch so that those that didn't match are displayed – and the matching ones are hidden.

Basic steps

☐ **To restore the full set:**

1 Open the **View** menu.

2 Select **Show All Records**.

☐ **To switch found and hidden records:**

1 Open the **View** menu.

2 Select **Switch Hidden Records**.

	Customer	Amount Owing	Credit Limit	
1	Dodger & Bodger	£748.56	£500.00	
4	Acme Inc	£2,547.90	£2,000.00	
6				
7				
8				
9				
10				
11				

DEBTORS.WDB

Take note

After a Query has been aplied, you can only see those records that match the search requirements. If you produce a report now, only these records will be included in the output.

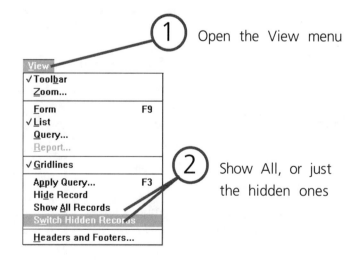

① Open the View menu

② Show All, or just the hidden ones

View
✓ Tool**b**ar
Zoom...

Form   F9
✓ **L**ist
Query...
Report...

✓ **G**ridlines

A**p**ply Query...   F3
Hi**d**e Record
Show **A**ll Records
S**w**itch Hidden Records

Headers and Footers...

Basic steps

□ **To delete a query:**

1 Open the **Tools** menu and select **Delete Query...**

2 Pick the name from the list and click **OK**.

□ **To reuse a query:**

1 Open the **View** menu and select **Apply Query...**

2 Pick the name from the list and click **OK**.

Take note

If you forgot to name your query – so that it is still called **Query7** or the like – use **Tools | Rename Query** to give it something more meaningful.

Deleting and reusing queries

Some queries are one-offs – you might want to find Aunty Flo's address to invite her to a christening. These should be deleted after use, so that they don't clutter up the system. Others queries are run regularly – the weekly chasing of debts, the monthly stock-taking. If you have named your queries clearly, you will be able to pick up these regulars and re-apply them without any further work.

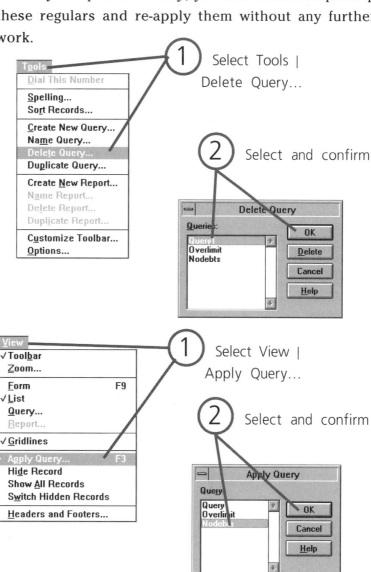

(1) Select Tools | Delete Query...

(2) Select and confirm

(1) Select View | Apply Query...

(2) Select and confirm

Reporting out

The database's report routines produce straightforward lists of the data held in the records. There is very little you can do about the layout, but you can control the content. You can:

● select the fields to be included in the reports,

● restrict the report to selected records, by applying a query,

● include a variety of summary statistics.

1 Open the **Tools** menu and select **Create New Report...** or click the **New Report** dialog box opens.

2 Type in a heading for your report. (N.B. the Header/Footer codes do not work here.)

3 Highlight a field that is to be included and click **Add >>**

4 Repeat until all the wanted fields have been copied into the Fields in report list.

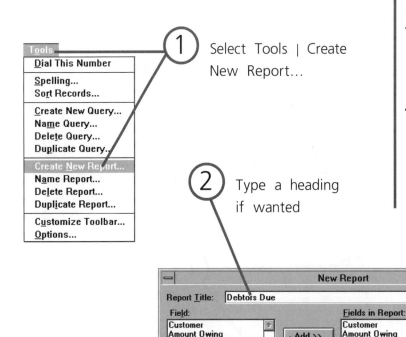

Select Tools | Create New Report...

Type a heading if wanted

Add the fields to the in Report list

5 If you have added one by mistake, highlight it and click **Remove**

6 Click **OK** to move on to the **Report Statistics** dialog box.

7 Select a field for which you want a summary figure.

8 Select the summary **Statistics**.

9 Repeat 7 and 8 for all desired summaries.

10 If you want the statistics **Under each column**, check this option.

11 Click **OK**.

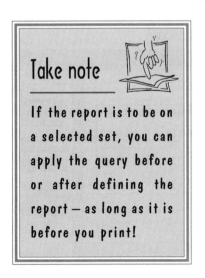

Take note

If the report is to be on a selected set, you can apply the query before or after defining the report — as long as it is before you print!

⑦ Select a field

⑧ Select a summary

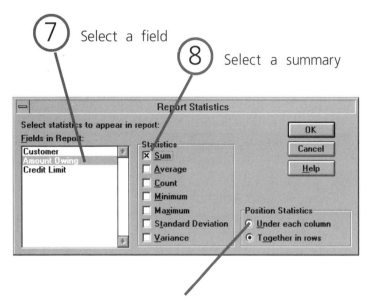

Under each column is useful where you have several columns of values to be counted or totalled

DEBTORS.WDB	A	B	C	D
Title				Debtors Due
Title				
Headings	**Customer**	**Amount Owing**	**Credit Limit**	
Headings				
Record	=Customer	=Amount Owing	=Credit Limit	
Summary				
Summary	TOTAL Amount Owing:		=SUM(Amount O	

The Report view is based on the List. You may well have to widen the columns to make room for the headings and for the data in the fields. Titles and headings can be changed if necessary, using the normal editing methods.

Improved outputs

The Report view gives you very little idea of how the report will look on paper. To see that, you must use Print Preview. Make a habit of doing this, as Works does a fairly basic job on layout. Having previewed, adjust widths, format and add any extra items in Report view.

1 Adjust **Column Widths** to fit the headings, or the longest item in each field.

2 **Format** the text to make headings stand out better.

3 Add **Borders** or **Patterns** if you want to focus on particular items.

4 Check with **Print Preview**!

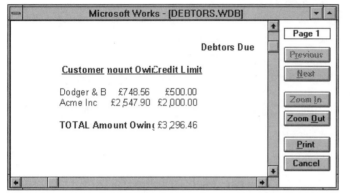

Before

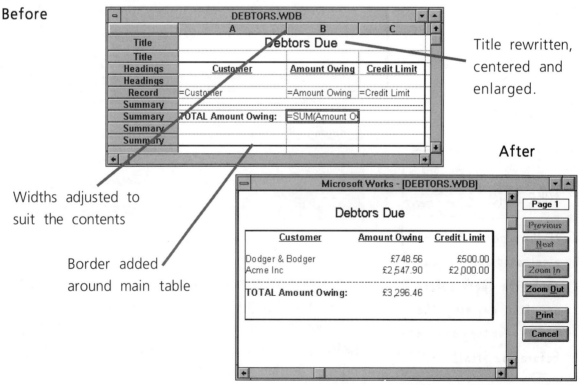

Title rewritten, centered and enlarged.

After

Widths adjusted to suit the contents

Border added around main table

118

Basic steps

□ **To name a report:**

1 Open the **Tools** menu and select **Name Report...**

2 Highlight the report in the list.

3 Type its new **Name** in the slot at the bottom.

4 Click **Rename**.

5 Click **OK**.

□ **To reuse a report:**

1 Open the **View** menu and select **Reports...**

2 Highlight the one you want to use.

3 Click **OK**.

Naming and reusing reports

For reasons best known to the designers, you are not given you the opportunity to name a report, as you are a query. You are likely to reuse report designs, just as you will reuse queries – in fact, you well have a report for each query. If they have meaningful names, if will be easier to find them again when you next want them.

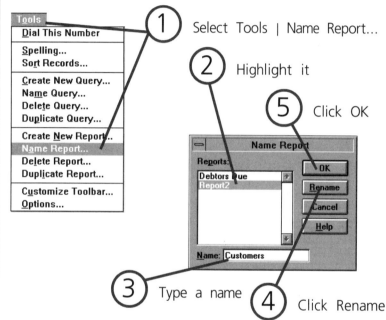

Select Tools | Name Report...

② Highlight it

⑤ Click OK

③ Type a name

④ Click Rename

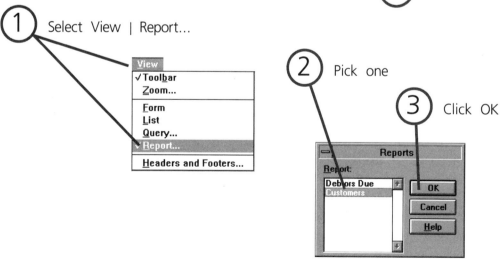

① Select View | Report...

② Pick one

③ Click OK

Summary

- ❏ A database is a collection of **records**, with **fields** holding the separate details for each record.

- ❏ If you organise your data before you start to create the database, you will save yourself trouble.

- ❏ **Field names** and text labels can be typed anywhere on a form. If the text ends with a colon, it is a field name.

- ❏ Fields' **widths**, and their locations can be adjusted at any time without affecting any data they may hold.

- ❏ Fonts and alignments can be set in the usual way, but borders only apply to individual items. If you want a box around a some items, **Insert** a **Rectangle**.

- ❏ **List view** looks and acts much the same as a spreadsheet.

- ❏ **Queries** search for those records that have particular values in given fields. The comparison can be with actual values, or the values in another field.

- ❏ After a query has been applied you can only see those records that match. To see the rest again, use **View | Show All Records**.

- ❏ To reuse a Query, select it from the **Apply Query** list.

- ❏ **Reports** list the chosen fields for the current set of records. They can include summary values.

- ❏ The appearance of the report can be adjusted by editing it in **Report view**.

9 Working together

Inserting objects

Works Charts, tables, Draw, Clip and WordArt graphics, database fields and other objects from other Windows applications can be inserted into word processor documents and database forms. Whatever the type of object, the techniques are much the same. In these pages the objects are ClipArt pictures .

When first inserted, an object will push any existing text out of its way and sit by itself on the left of the page, as above. This is its *In-Line* Wrap mode, and in this you can change its size, drag it to another line and set its Left-Right alignment. The alternative *Absolute* Wrap mode gives you more flexibility. In this mode it can be embedded within text, and positioned anywhere on the page.

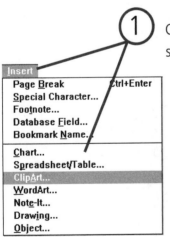

① Open the Insert menu and select the object type

Insert

Page **B**reak	**C**trl+Enter
Special Character...	
Foo**t**note...	
Database **F**ield...	
Bookmark **N**ame...	
Chart...	
S**p**readsheet/Table...	
Clip**A**rt...	
WordArt...	
Note-**I**t...	
Dra**w**ing...	
Object...	

□ **To insert an object:**

1 Place the insertion pointer where you want the object to go.

2 Open the **Insert** menu and select the type of object.

3 Wait for a moment for the object to settle in.

□ **To switch Wrap modes:**

1 Highlight the object.

2 Open the **Format** menu and select **Picture/Object**.

3 Bring the **TextWrap** panel to the front and click on the **In-Line** or **Absolute** icon as required.

Take note

Objects can be resized or moved with the usual mouse methods (see *Adjusting the layout*, page 106), but can be adjusted more accurately through the Format Picture/Object dialog box.

☐ **To set an exact size:**

1 Highlight the object.

2 Open the **Format** menu and select **Picture/Object**.

3 Bring the **Size** panel to the front and type in the required values for either **Size** or **Scale**.

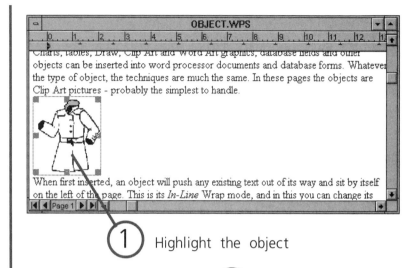

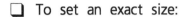 Highlight the object

Select Format| Picture/Object

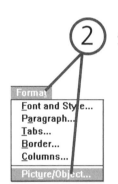

Set the Wrap mode

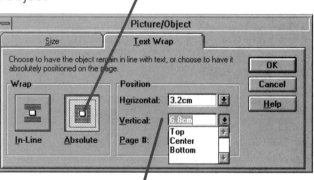

Horizontal and Vertical positions can be set on this panel

Set Scale or Width and Height

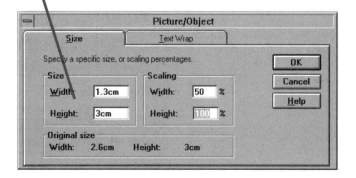

Tip

There are toolbar buttons to insert all the Works objects.

ClipArt

The Clip Art Gallery at first only contains the small set of graphics supplied with Works, but you can easily add your own. The Gallery can handle graphics produced by different packages and stored in different formats, and there are no limitations on size. They are displayed in the Gallery as 'thumbnails', but are restored to their normal size when inserted into a document.

1 Select **Insert | Clip Art** or click to open the **Gallery**.

2 Click **Options...** to open the Options panel.

3 To add selected pictures, click **Add**

Selecting a category makes it easier to find pictures – especially if you have added a lot of your own

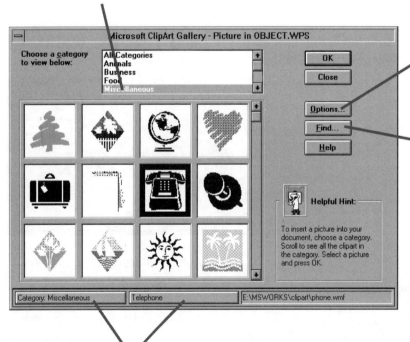

② Click Options

Use this if you have a lot of pictures. It can find them by their Description name

Clicking either of these Category and Description buttons will bring up the Edit Picture panel, where you can change the picture's category or description.

Tip

To add every picture stored on any one or all of your drives, click the Refresh button — it's quicker than Adding them.

4 In the **Add Clipart** dialox box, set the **Drive** and **Directory** to get to your files.

5 If you are only interested in a certain **Type of file**, select it from the bottom slot.

6 Highlight a file in the list.

7 Click **OK**.

8 At the next panel, select a **Category** for the picture.

9 Type a **Description**, if wanted.

10 Click [**Add**]

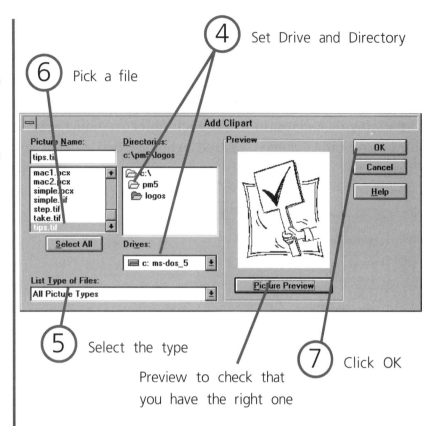

④ Set Drive and Directory

⑥ Pick a file

⑤ Select the type

Preview to check that you have the right one

⑦ Click OK

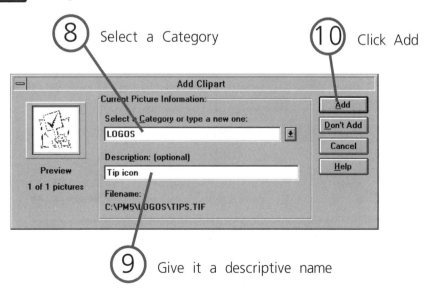

⑧ Select a Category

⑩ Click Add

⑨ Give it a descriptive name

MS-Draw

If you are used to Paintbrush, the first thing to realise is that Draw is different. With Paintbrush, anything you add to the picture covers whatever is beneath and becomes a permanent part of the image - just as if you were painting on canvas. In Draw, each object remains separate and can be moved, resized, recoloured or deleted at any time

Basic steps

1 Open the **Insert** menu and select **Drawing** or click

2 Select a tool to create an object.

3 Adjust its size, position colours and font style as necessary.

4 Repeat steps 2 and 3 to create your image.

5 Open the **File** menu and select **Update** to copy the picture into you document file.

6 Open the **File** menu and select **Exit and Return to...**

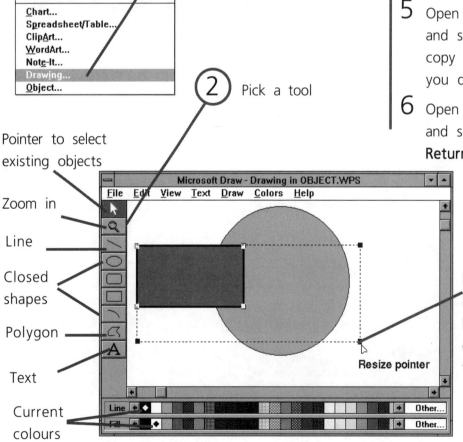

① Select Insert | Drawing

② Pick a tool

Pointer to select existing objects

Zoom in

Line

Closed shapes

Polygon

Text

Current colours

Hold a corner block to resize. Drag anywhere else on the object to move it.

Resize pointer

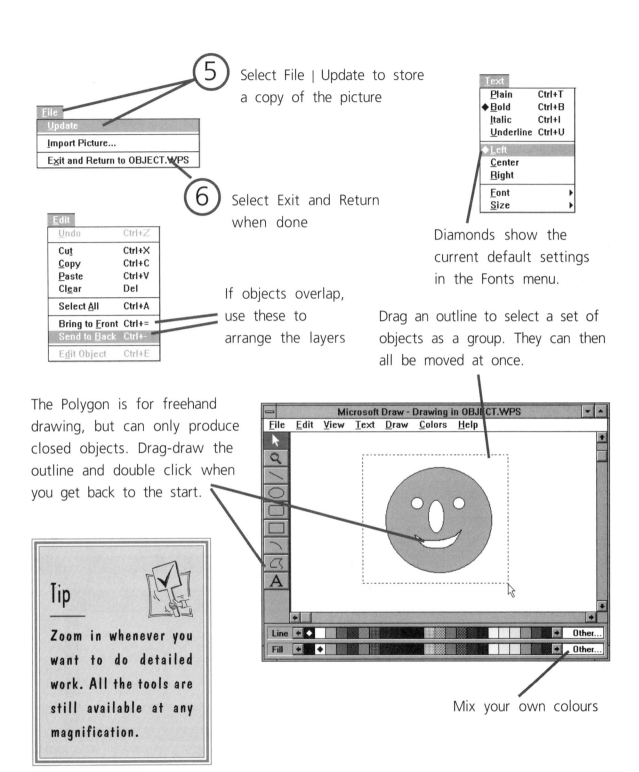

⑤ Select File | Update to store a copy of the picture

File
Update
Import Picture...
E_xit and Return to OBJECT.WPS

⑥ Select Exit and Return when done

Text
Plain   Ctrl+T
◆ Bold   Ctrl+B
Italic   Ctrl+I
Underline Ctrl+U
◆ Left
Center
Right
Font   ▶
Size   ▶

Diamonds show the current default settings in the Fonts menu.

Edit
Undo   Ctrl+Z
Cut   Ctrl+X
Copy   Ctrl+C
Paste   Ctrl+V
Clear   Del
Select All   Ctrl+A
Bring to Front Ctrl+=
Send to Back Ctrl+-
Edit Object   Ctrl+E

If objects overlap, use these to arrange the layers

Drag an outline to select a set of objects as a group. They can then all be moved at once.

The Polygon is for freehand drawing, but can only produce closed objects. Drag-draw the outline and double click when you get back to the start.

Tip

Zoom in whenever you want to do detailed work. All the tools are still available at any magnification.

Microsoft Draw - Drawing in OBJECT.WPS
File   Edit   View   Text   Draw   Colors   Help

Line
Fill

Other...
Other...

Mix your own colours

127

WordArt

With WordArt, text can be rotated, distorted, shadowed and patterened. The process is fiddly, but it does allow you to make a real splash with text. You could put it to good use it for invitations, adverts, posters, newsletters and the like.

The system has a couple of flaws:

● you cannot resize of the object from within WordArt, and a different effect may require a different size;

● the proportions of the object stay constant, even though the text may occupy only a small part of it if it has been rotated or curved

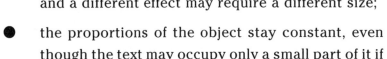

Select Insert | WordArt

Type your text

Click Update

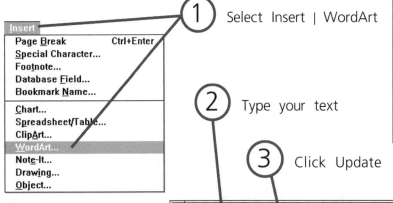

Displays font sets from which you can select special characters

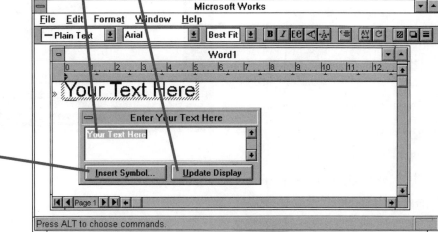

Basic steps

1 Open the **Insert** menu and select **WordArt** or click 🄰

2 Type your text into the WordArt window

3 Click **Update Display** to write it to the page.

4 Point and click back into your document.

5 Select the WordArt object and resize it.

6 Double click on the object to return to WordArt to set the effects. (Expect to do steps 5 and 6 several times before you have finished!)

The buttons

Ee makes lower case letters the same height as capitals.

◁ rotates the text through 90 degrees.

⊿Å makes the text expand to fill the shape.

AV↔ sets the tracking – the spacing between characters.

C sets rotation and arc anges through the Special Effects panel. (See right.)

▨ sets the fill patterns for the letters.

▢ sets the shadow style (See right.)

≡ sets the style of the outline of the letters.

This has been curved, with the arc flattened to 30°, then given a fill pattern, thin outline and simple black shadow.

Text effects

These can all be set from the toolbar – either from the buttons or the three drop-down lists. The font and size lists as are normal, except that there is a **Best Fit** size – generally the best option. The new list is on the left.

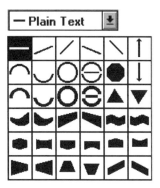

This sets the overall shape made by the text. The shape may well be much smaller than the object's outline – be prepared to enlarge it.

With curved text, a smaller Arc Angle flattens the curve.

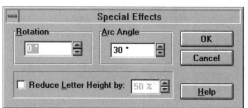

The on-the-ground shadows do not work well with shaped text. Keep these for straight text.

WordArt stands out

Note-It

This adds an icon, with a note attached. Double-clicking on the icon makes the note pop up in the top left of the screen.You might use them for pinning comments onto a document that is being passed (electronically) around the office, or for putting reminders or brief explanatory notes beside fields in a database.

Notes can be moved, resized and deleted, just like any other object. You can also edit their text and icon.

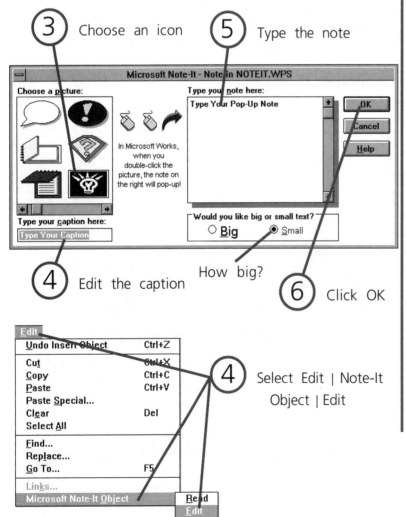

Choose an icon

Type the note

Edit the caption

How big?

Click OK

Select Edit | Note-It Object | Edit

❑ **To add a note:**

1 Place the insertion point where you want to add the note.

2 Open the **Insert** menu and select **Note-It** or click 📝

3 Scroll through the **icons** and select a suitable one.

4 Change the **caption** - if you do not want one, then at least erase the prompt.

5 Type your **note**.

6 Click **OK**.

❑ **To edit a note:**

1 Select the note's icon.

2 Open the **Edit** menu and select **Microsoft Note-It Object**, then **Edit** from the sub-menu. This takes you back into the Note-It dialog box.

Linked objects

Basic steps

1 Open the **Insert** menu and select **Object...**

2 If you want to **Create new**, pick the source application from the list.

3 Wait for the application to load.

4 Within the application, remember to use **File | Update** before **File | Exit and Return**.

A *linked* object is one that was created by another application, and that retains its connection to that application within its Works document. Double-clicking onthe object (apart from the Note-It icons) will usually activate the link and open the original application so that the object can be edited.

This linking can be extended beyond the Microsoft add-ons to any other piece of software that can handle the Windows link mechanism – and almost all new Windows applications can do this.

When you insert an object, you will be offered the choice of creating a new one or using an existing file. Only take this second route if you know that the file can be linked.

Click here to get to a panel where you can browse through the system to find your file.

The list should display all the suitable applications on your system.

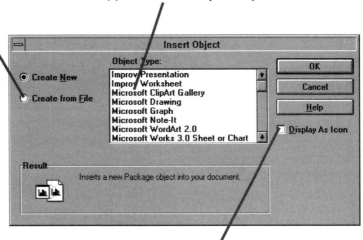

Take note

Linking objects uses a lot of memory. Unless you have got loads of RAM, expect to have to wait while Windows swaps memory to and from the hard disk.

Use *icon* displays where you want a convenient link to another file, but do not want it to be visible in your document.

Charts and tables

The formatting facilities in the spreadsheet are not bad, but if you want a really good-looking report from a spreadsheet, the simplest solution is to write it in the word processor and insert tables and charts from the sheet. To be able to do this, the ranges that form the tables of data must have been given names within the spreadsheet. The charts may still be called Chart1, Chart2 and so on, though meaningful names for these will also make them easier to find when you are inserting.

❑ **To insert a chart or table:**

1 Open the spreadsheet containing the chart.

2 Return to the word processor document by clicking on it or by picking its name from the **Window** menu.

3 Open the **Insert** menu and select **Chart** or **Spreadsheet / Table**

4 Select the spreadsheet from the left hand list.

5 Select the chart or range from the list on the right.

6 Click **OK**.

You can also create new charts from this panel

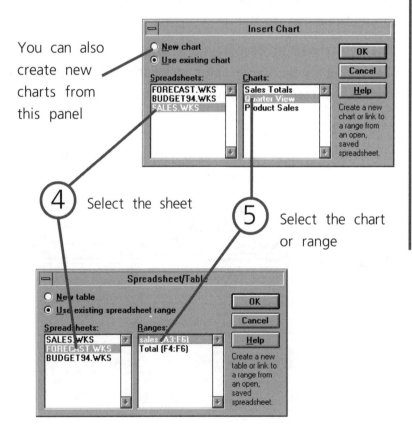

④ Select the sheet

⑤ Select the chart or range

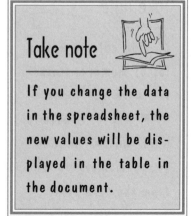

Take note

If you change the data in the spreadsheet, the new values will be displayed in the table in the document.

Mail merge

1 Start writing your standard letter in the word processor. Stop when you reach the point where you want to pull in data.

2 Open the **Insert** menu and select **Database Field..**

3 If the database is open it will be shown as the **Current database**. Move to step

4 Click **Database...** to open the **Choose Database** panel.

With Mail merge, you take information from a database and slot it into a standard layout to produce mailing labels or personalized letters. It's a trick that Reader's Digest discovered 20 years ago and other marketing departments have been using ever since. With Works, a mail merge is simple to organise. The difficult part is composing a letter that people do not throw straight into the waste paper basket.

① Stop when you want some data

② Select Insert | Database Field

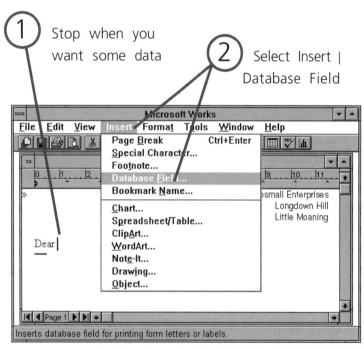

Tip

Try and get the fields in the right place at the start. They are not as easy to move as other objects.

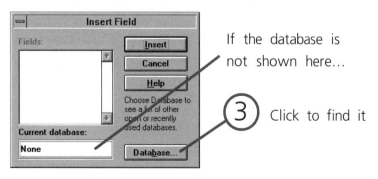

If the database is not shown here...

③ Click to find it

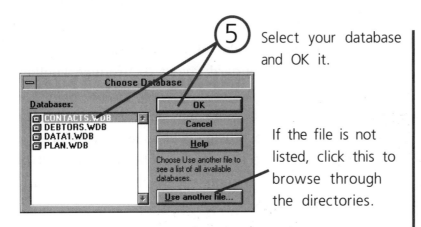

Select your database and OK it.

If the file is not listed, click this to browse through the directories.

5 In the **Choose Database** dialog box, you will see a list of those in the current directory. If the one you want is there, highlight it and click **OK**.

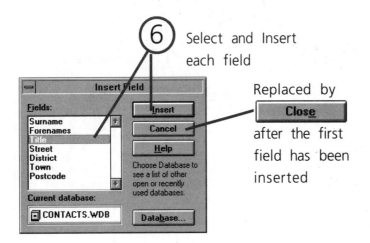

Select and Insert each field

Replaced by

after the first field has been inserted

6 Back in the **Insert Field** dialog box, highlight a field and click **Insert**

7 If you want other fields straight after the first, highlight and insert them.

8 Click **Close** when done.

Two fields inserted into the text

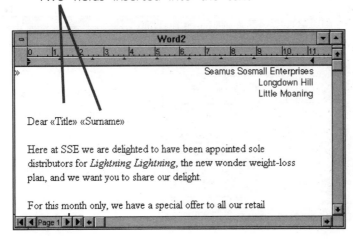

Basic steps

❏ **To delete a field:**

1 If you are still in the **Insert Field** dialog box, wait until you have returned to the document.

2 Select and delete the field name as you would any other text.

❏ To move a field:

1 Select the name and enclosing «chevrons»

2 Drag and drop into its new place.

❏ **To print:**

1 Select **File | Print**.

2 When the **Choose Database** dialog box opens, select the one you want.

3 Carry on printing as normal.

A database field 'object' is simply another piece of text as far as editing goes. You can move them, if necessary – but do take care to select the «chevrons» that surround the names, and do not edit the names in any way.

When you start to Print the mail letters, you will first be asked for the database. There is a point to this. You may have several databases with a common field structure, each concerned with a different category of people, and want to use the same letter on any one of them.

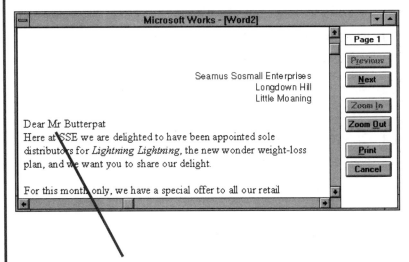

A Print Preview of the mail merge letter, showing the first Title and Surname pulled in from the database.

Summary

- ❏ Objects can be **inserted** into word processor documents and database forms. Double-clicking on them or using the **Edit | Object** command will reopen the application that created them.

- ❏ Objects can be resized and repositioned. They can sit in lines free of text or have text wrapped round them.

- ❏ You can add other pictures to the **ClipArt** Gallery.

- ❏ **Draw** is an object-base graphics package. With it you can build up pictures out of lines, circles, rectangles and closed polygons.

- ❏ **WordArt** can produce text that is curved, shaped, stretched, shadowed and patterned.

- ❏ Note-It lets you place icons, with pop-up notes, on your documents.

- ❏ Objects produced by other Windows applications can be **linked** into your files.

- ❏ **Charts** and **Tables**, from open spreadsheets, can be inserted. As with other linked objects, the display in the document will be updated if the spreadsheet is edited.

- ❏ By inserting **Database Fields**, you can create mail merge documents.

10 Working on-line

Setting up

Working on-line is getting easier, though you will still meet more jargon here than in any other application. But Works does its best to simplify the process and you can often ignore much of the jargon. If you have the phone number and the basic communications settings of the comms service that you want to access, then you should be able to get on-line – the terminal settings may need tweaking to get the best display, but at least you should get through.

❑ **To start a new file:**

1 Type the **Phone number,** including spaces and dashes (-) if you like.

2 Type a **Name** for your reference.

3 Click **OK**.

4 The system will try to connect you. You might be best to **Cancel** and adjust the settings before going on-line.

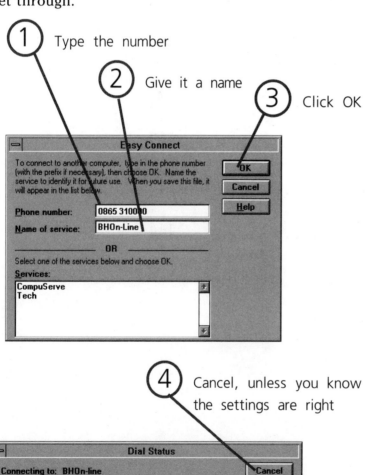

① Type the number

② Give it a name

③ Click OK

Easy Connect

To connect to another computer, type in the phone number (with the prefix if necessary), then choose OK. Name the service to identify it for future use. When you save this file, it will appear in the list below.

OK
Cancel
Help

Phone number: 0865 310000
Name of service: BHOn-Line

_____ OR _____

Select one of the services below and choose OK.

Services:
CompuServe
Tech

④ Cancel, unless you know the settings are right

Dial Status

Connecting to: BHOn-line   Cancel
Status   Help
Initializing modem   2

Take note

If you try to connect and get a Modem failed message, set a slower Baud rate and try again. Works seems to take an optimistic view fo what a modem can do.

Basic steps

Communication settings

❏ **To adjust settings:**

1 Open the **Settings** menu and select **Communications**, or click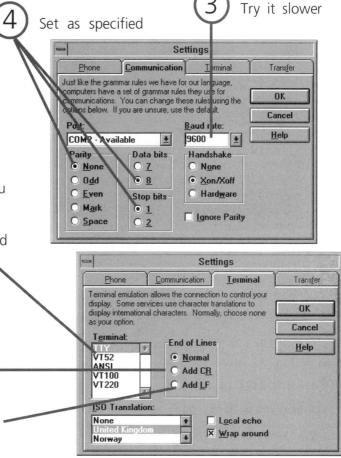

2 The system should have detected the correct **Port** for your modem. If it says Available, leave it.

3 Reduce the **Baud rate**, if necessary.

4 Use the **Parity/Bits** settings specified by the comms service.

Unless you know what is needed, leave the Terminal settings until you have been on-line.

The **Terminals** are all text-based and will work much the same – the difference is mainly in the special characters that they recognise.

Add CR (Carriage Return) if you find incoming text disappearing off the right of the screen.

Add LF (Line Feed), if it overwrites, rather than scrolling up the screen.

You will normally only have to adjust two settings:

Baud rate – the speed at which data travels. If you cannot connect at the current rate, take it a step down and try again. The faster it is , the lower your phone bills will be.

Parity/Bits settings – The two most common combinations can be set from the toolbar.

⬛ 7,e,1 - 7 bits, Even Parity, 1 stop bit;

⬛ 8,n,1 - 8 bits, No Parity, 1 stop bit

④ Set as specified   ③ Try it slower

139

Transfer settings

The Transfer protocol governs how you maintain a connection with the computer at the other end of the line. XModem is the default and the most common. Only change this if told to by the comms service.

The one part of this panel that does need your attention is the **Directory**. When you are capturing or sending text while on-line, you do not want to have to waste time changing the directory.

1 Switch to the **Transfer** panel or click 🖻 on the toolbar

2 Set the **Protocol** if one is specified by the comms service.

3 Click **Directory...**

4 Choose the directory in which your comms files will be stored.

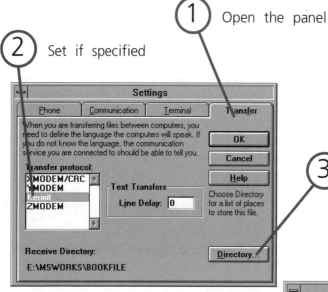

① Open the panel

② Set if specified

③ Click to choose

④ Set the Drive and Directory

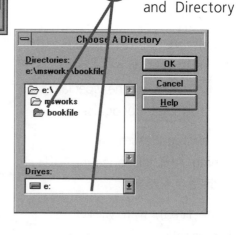

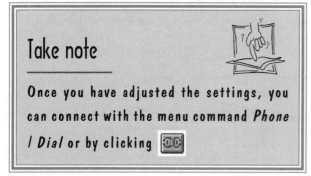

Take note

Once you have adjusted the settings, you can connect with the menu command *Phone / Dial* or by clicking 📳

Capturing text

1 Open the **Tools** menu and select **Capture Text...** or click

2 Set the **Directory** if you omitted to do this earlier.

3 Type in a **Filename**.

4 Click **OK**.

5 Set the incoming text flowing.

6 When you reach the end, open the **Tools** menu and select **End Capture Text**.

The key to successful working on-line is to do as much as possible *off*-line. All the time that you are on-line, you are clocking up phone charges, and perhaps service charges as well. You cannot read the text at the same speed that it comes in – unless you are a very quick reader and have a very slow modem – and you certainly cannot type as fast as it can be sent!

Any time that you have a chunk of text coming down the line, that doesn't require an immediate reply, capture it into a file and deal with it later.

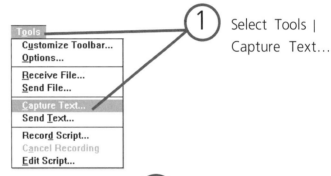

① Select Tools | Capture Text...

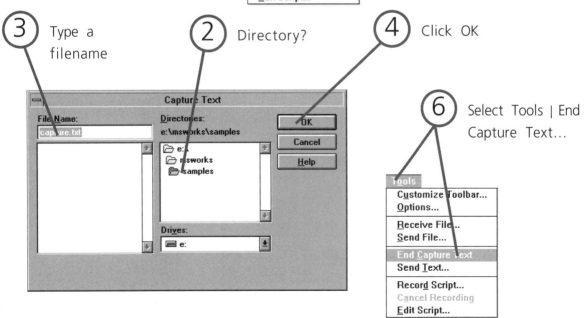

③ Type a filename

② Directory?

④ Click OK

⑥ Select Tools | End Capture Text...

Sending text

A fast typist can type 100 words or about 600 characters a minute. A fast modem can send over 900 characters a *second*, or 50,000+ a minute. Even the slowest modem can shift 1800 characters a minute.If you are sending mail, or have a long comment to add to a forum, or a long signing-in routine, prepare it off-line.

Type your mail in the word processor. When you save it, specify **Text** as the type of file, and store it in your comms directory.

Basic steps

1 Prepare you text file(s) before you start.

2 At any point during the comms session, when it is waiting for a keyboard input, open the **Tools** menu and select **Send Text...** or click

3 Switch to the right **directory** if necessary.

4 Select your **file**.

5 Click **OK**.

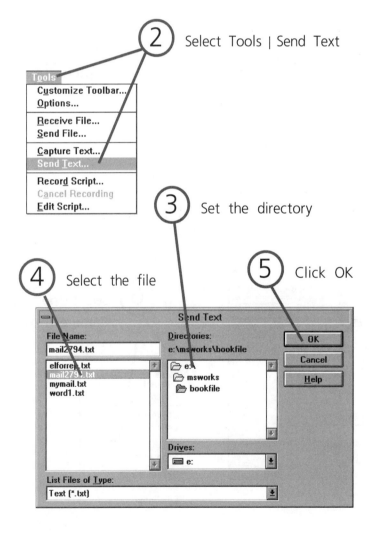

② Select Tools | Send Text

③ Set the directory

④ Select the file

⑤ Click OK

Tip

Clear used and unwanted files out of your comms directory regularly, to make it easier to find the one you want to send in the session.

Basic steps

1 Sign off to close your on-line connection.

2 Open the **Phone** menu and select **Hang Up**.

When you sign off from your comms service, it closes the connection to them, but does not put the phone back on the hook. Don't forget to hang up! Likewise, don't hang up without first signing off, or you could be running up connection charges even though you are not there.

① Select Phone | Hang Up

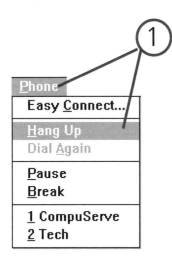

```
Phone
   Easy Connect...
   Hang Up
   Dial Again
   Pause
   Break
   1 CompuServe
   2 Tech
```

Goodbye

This is where I sign off. The coverage of Communications has been brief, but this is a small book and Works is a big package. Writing this has been a struggle to get a quart into a pint pot. I hope that it has been enough to get you started, and that you are now ready to explore Works — and comms — in greater depth.

Summary

❑ Apart from the **Parity/Bits** and **Baud rate**, most of the default settings should not need changing.

❑ If you are having trouble reading the screen, check what **Terminal** settings your comms service can deal with, and pick one of those.

❑ For the most efficient use of phone time, you should handle as much text as possible *off-line*.

❑ Use **Capture Text** to store incoming text in a file.

❑ Use **Send Text** for anything much more than responses to interactive prompts.

❑ Don't forget to sign off and **hang up** at the end of a session.

Index